FAMILY WORSHIP
FOR THE THANKSGIVING SEASON

OTHER AVAILABLE TITLES IN THIS SERIES
FROM THE PEN AND HEART OF RAY RHODES, JR.

Family Worship for the Reformation Season

Family Worship for the Christmas Season

OTHER PROJECTED TITLES IN THIS SERIES

Family Worship for the Easter Season

Family Worship for the Summer Season

FAMILY WORSHIP
FOR
THE THANKSGIVING SEASON

Ray Rhodes, Jr.

SOLID GROUND CHRISTIAN BOOKS
BIRMINGHAM, ALABAMA USA

Solid Ground Christian Books
PO Box 660132
Vestavia Hills AL 35266
205-443-0311
sgcb@charter.net
solid-ground-books.com

FAMILY WORSHIP FOR THE THANKSGIVING SEASON
by Ray Rhodes, Jr.

First Solid Ground Edition October 2009

Cover design by Borgo Design, Tuscaloosa, AL

Scripture references in this book are taken from the New King James Version of the Holy Bible.

ISBN: 978-159925-224-7

Dedication

To Rachel, our first born.

Your determination and godly passion for Jesus are all wrapped in beauty of God's grace. Your pursuit of Christ challenges me. Though we now coach basketball together--I fondly remember your pony tail bouncing as you ran up and down the court as the point guard for the Wildcats. You led the way then and you lead the way now helping our family to think of the growth of God's kingdom around the world. The ball is now a globe and your vision is beyond the scoreboard and embraces the nations. On this, our twentieth Thanksgiving Day together, I thank our great God for adorning our home with His grace displayed through you. You are my daughter, friend and sister in Christ.

And knowing how much you enjoy Jane Austen...

"If I loved you less, I might be able to talk about it more."
Jane Austen

Love, Daddy

September, 2009

Special Thanks

To: My wife Lori. The few days that we were alone together to finish this book were the best days of the past year. Thank you for making the time and for being my very best friend.

To: My daughters Rachel, Hannah, Sarah, Mary and Lydia. From "rough housing" and "ice-cream man" games to worshiping God together—and all of the holiday gatherings—I love you all.

To: Our parents and siblings. Don't you wish we had recordings of all of the table talk over the years? Well...maybe not. It is hard to believe that I have more gray hair than you all.

To: My Editor in Chief: David Bailey (my long time friend and editor of all my books thus far). You have been my friend through the mountains and the valleys.

To: Editors, Lori and Rachel Rhodes. I appreciate your notes, suggestions and corrections. Thanks for liking the book even after so many readings.

To: Publisher, Mike Gaydosh. Thanks for the inspiration to keep writing these books. Three down and nine to go!

To: Grace Community Church. You are very patient with your "scattered, smothered, and covered" Pastor. Thanks for embracing Nourished in the Word Ministries and for supporting me in this ministry of our church.

To: The Georgia Baptist Conference Center, Toccoa, GA. Thanks to director Bill Wheeler and Georgia Baptists who provided me with a two-night stay that was helpful in writing this book (www.toccoa.gabaptist.org).

Table of Contents

Family Worship for the Thanksgiving Season

Over 40 million Americans will travel fifty or more miles during the Thanksgiving holiday to visit with family and friends. With the growth of America since its founding has also come the scattering of families across the land. Thanksgiving Day calls families to journey "over the river and through the wood" to sit around the table, enjoy a meal and remember days gone by. In the homes of Christians, Thanksgiving serves as another opportunity to recount the faithfulness of God and to give Him thanks.

I pray that this book will be a help to you as you lead your family to worship God. Each day includes a Scripture reading, historical glimpse and theological thought. Read these sections with your family and consider adding a hymn and a prayer of thanksgiving as a part of your regular family worship activities.

The First Thanksgiving

Several streams converged that have helped to form the Thanksgiving Day tradition that Americans celebrate on the fourth Thursday of November each year. Most prominent is the gathering of Pilgrims and Indians at Plymouth in 1621. This celebration followed a bountiful harvest and the best conditions that the Pilgrims had enjoyed since touching the shores of their new home. Soon after arriving at Cape Cod, Massachusetts, in November of 1620, the Pilgrims began exploring the New England coastline and they came face to face with the brutality of a North Eastern winter. With the cold, wind, snow, and rain and without adequate shelter, their suffering was increased and their number was reduced. By April of 1621 only 51 of the 102 original settlers were alive. Out of the 51 there were only twenty men and eight women. The rest were children. From that great grief came the provision of God. In God's grace, friendship with Indians was cultivated, vegetables were planted, trading was established, homes were built and life improved. For three days in the fall of 1621, the Pilgrims gave thanks to God and with Indian friends they ate and danced. This celebration, in my opinion, is the foundational event for our modern Thanksgiving Day. Of course the Pilgrims did not know that such a tradition would follow. Though they suffered much on the soil that we now call home, their story is one of thanksgiving to God for His provision.

Though there were days of thanksgiving at various times and for various reasons from the early days of the settling of America, there was missing a formally recognized National Day of Thanksgiving. That would change—primarily through the influence of a lady by the name of Sarah Josepha Hale.

Sarah Josepha Hale

Sarah was born in 1788 while memories of the Revolutionary War were still fresh on everyone's mind and the fires of patriotism were burning bright.

In their early years Sarah and her brother were homeschooled by their mother. College was not a possibility for a young lady in Sarah's day (interestingly Sarah would later help to open doors for women to receive a college education). Educational limitations were no match for Sarah's desire to learn. Her passion for knowledge is evident throughout her life. Though she had only a few books, she studied them intensely. She read the Bible and *The Pilgrim's Progress* (both common in the homes of early Americans). Her brother Horatio instructed her with his books from college and by his help she learned Latin, advanced math and other disciplines.

By the time Sarah was 18 she was teaching school and her gifts were obvious. She was a faithful student, a devoted Christian and she was growing mightily in character.

Sarah, at age 25, married a popular young lawyer named David Hale. He was a great encouragement to her and she loved him dearly. Both enjoyed reading and study. Sarah wrote, "We commenced, soon after our marriage, a system of study and reading, which we pursued while he lived. The hours allotted were from eight o'clock until ten—two hours in twenty-four. How I enjoyed those hours! In this manner we studied French, Botany...and obtained some knowledge of Mineralogy, Geology, etc., besides pursuing a long and instructive course of reading. In all our mental pursuits, it seemed the aim of my husband to enlighten my reason, strengthen my judgment, and give me confidence in my own powers of mind, which he estimated more highly than I did. I equaled him in imagination, but in no other faculty. Yet the approbation which he bestowed on my talents has been of great encouragement to me in attempting the duties which were to be my portion." [1]

Imagine what might happen in your home if you set aside the television, computer and cell-phone for a couple of hours each evening and pulled out books for you and your wife to read and study together. Imagine the impact on your children.

David and Sarah had four children and she was pregnant with their fifth child when David had a stroke and died. Two weeks after his death their fifth child was born. Sarah was 34. Sarah referred to their marriage, "To me, the period of our union was one of unbroken happiness".[2] She faced many challenges after the loss of her beloved husband. There was not much of an inheritance left for her and she was a widow with a home full of children. Somehow she must find a way to provide for her family.

Assisted in publishing by some of her husband's friends she wrote two books of poems. The second book contained the famous children's poem, *Mary Had a Little Lamb*.

Sarah continued to write and eventually she became the editor of what would become the most influential ladies magazine in America—*Godey's Ladies Book*. She would serve as the editor of *Godey's* for almost fifty years. This publication contained recipes, moral fiction, art, poetry and advice. Here she gave helpful counsel to ladies on issues related to womanhood, including being a good wife, etiquette, dress and education. Sarah was not a feminist, but with an eye towards godliness, worked tirelessly to advance women—especially in education. It was also through *Godey's Ladies Book* that Sarah gave her most public attention to the establishment of a national Thanksgiving Day.

Sarah wrote an important novel, *Northwood*, in which she described life in New England in the early 1800's. She wrote, "We have too few holidays. Thanksgiving like the Fourth of July should be considered a national festival and observed by all our people..." This was written in 1827. In *Northwood* she devotes two chapters to Thanksgiving including sections on the Thanksgiving worship service and describes in detail the food and decorations for the family celebration.
In 1846 she stepped up her efforts to promote a national Thanksgiving Day. It would take 17 years before President

Lincoln would issue a proclamation for such a day (1863). During those preceding years she would write many hundreds of letters (by hand) along with her editorials promoting Thanksgiving Day.

In 1853 in *Godey's Lady's Book* her vision became evident. She imagined a day where, "...millions of people sitting down, as it were, together to a feast of joy and thankfulness..."[3] She also had a vision for the kinds of foods that would be enjoyed (such as duck, ham, pudding and especially roasted turkey and pumpkin pie).[4]

After many years of writing and promoting her passion for Thanksgiving and arguing for the benefits of such a day (reuniting family, remembering God's faithfulness and strengthening the unity of the nation) she wrote a letter to President Abraham Lincoln requesting his consideration for such a day. The result is the now famous and beautifully written Presidential Thanksgiving Proclamation of 1863.

Though Lincoln was not the first President to issue a Thanksgiving Day Proclamation (that was Washington in 1798), his was the one that would result in the annual observance on the fourth Thursday in November as the national day of Thanksgiving.

Since Lincoln's Thanksgiving proclamation in 1863 there has been an unbroken succession of such Presidential proclamations and a National Thanksgiving Day connected with the fourth Thursday in November (however, read about the Thanksgivings of 1939-41). The author of *Mary Had a Little Lamb* is to be given much credit for our national holiday.

Ruth Finley in *The Lady of Godey's: Sarah Josepha Hale* lists in chapter one a number of Hale's accomplishments. Below are just a few.

❖ She was the early champion of elementary education for girls equal to that of boys and of higher education for women.

❖ She helped organize Vassar College, the first school of collegiate rank for girls.

❖ She demanded for housekeeping the dignity of a profession and put the term "domestic science" into the language.

❖ She was the first to stress the necessity of physical training for her sex.

❖ She organized, and for many years, was president of, the Seaman's Aid, establishing the first Sailors' Home.

❖ She sent out the first women medical missionaries.

❖ She raised the money that finished Bunker Hill Monument.

❖ She rescued the movement to preserve Mount Vernon as a national memorial.

❖ She was the author of some two- dozen books and hundreds of poems, including the best-known children's rhyme in the English language—*Mary Had a Little Lamb*.

❖ She was the first woman editor in this country and for more than forty years presided over the destiny of *Godey's Ladies Book*, the most widely circulated magazine of her times.

❖ She signed herself, "The Lady Editor."

❖ She was 38 years old before she started her writing career.[5]

The above list reflects some of her many accomplishments. Sarah was able to support her family and influence many people by picking up her pen and writing. Her pen proved to be very influential in the development and growth of the nation.

With all of the emphasis on Sarah's advancement of women in education, exercise, work and missions you might think that she was a forerunner to the modern feminist movement and should not garner the attention that she does in this book.

The excellent web site, www.pilgrimhall.org contains information on the Pilgrims, Thanksgiving and Sarah Hale. There you will find this statement:

"Sarah was, by no means a feminist. "God," she said "has given to man authority, to woman influence." A firm believer in separate spheres of activity for men and women, she was opposed to women's suffrage and did not believe that most of the masculine professions should be opened to women. She did, however, strongly believe that the status of women should be improved and that girls should be well educated." As she expressed in an 1856 editorial,

The companion of man should be able thoroughly to sympathize with him and her intellect should be as well developed as his. We do not believe in the mental inequality of the sexes, we believe that the man and the woman have each a work to do, for which they are specially qualified, and in which they are called to excel. Though the work is not the same, it is equally noble and demands an equal exercise of capacity.[6]

**We have been unable to do an in-depth study of Sarah Hale's theology. She professed to be a Christian and believed that Thanksgiving Day would be "the national pledge of the Christian faith." She believed that the gospel should be spread around the world and was instrumental in the promotion of women missionaries. Though she seemed to love the gospel, treasure the biblical institution of marriage, and understand the biblical distinctions between men and women, we are not sure as to the details of her overall theology. We were a bit concerned in our studies that she seemed to promote the spiritual superiority of women over men, however she did believe that women were to be submissive to men and that the spheres of women and men were different. Women could be missionaries, nurses, teachers, writers, etc. but were not to be political leaders nor occupy some of the other roles traditionally reserved for men. Perhaps at some time in the future we will do a study of the theology of Sarah Hale. For now simply enjoy her expressed love for God, country, morality and Thanksgiving

Day. Her character was such that there is much to learn from her. Though she contributed so much to the fabric of our nation, there is surprisingly little written information about her.

Interesting Quotes by Sarah Hale

The wife should be humble. She is dependent on her husband for the position she holds in society; she must rely on him for protection and support. She should look up to him with reverence as her earthly guardian and be obedient. Does any wife say her husband is not worthy of this honor! Then render it to the office with which God has invested him as head of the family; but use your privilege of motherhood to train our sons so that they may be worthy of this reverence and obedience from their wives. Thus, through your sufferings, the world may be made better; every faithful performance of private duty adds to the stock of public virtues."

"And man: should he not bear himself humbly, from the remembrance that to woman's loving care he is indebted for preservation during helpless infancy; that his mind takes its impress from her daily teachings; from her example he derives faith in those affections and virtues which are the life of the soul; that 'God has chosen the weak things of this world to confound the things which are mighty;' "

"Humility is a Christian virtue equally necessary for both sexes; by giving to each one particular endowments to which the other must pay honor, all cause for boasting is removed from both; each should seek to promote the other's happiness and glory, and then the true happiness and glory of both would be won."

"...to create is not man's greatest glory; it is to worship God in spirit and in truth. "

Quotes above taken from *Woman's Record: Distinguished Women.*[7]

Opening Statements

A proper regard for history is important— especially the history that is contained in the Bible (Psalm 78, Deuteronomy 6-8, I Corinthians 10:1-6).

It is important to keep post-New Testament history in a proper context. It is certainly possible to over-emphasize or under appreciate one's unique narrative—be it national or personal.

Though I draw heavily from the well of early American history in this book—I do so not as a foundation to our faith but as an illustration and application of how some believed and therefore lived. Conviction is not something that can simply be isolated and privatized in one's heart. It must be lived out. As you read the sketch of the Pilgrims (and others) contained herein you will note that they were people of conviction. They were like the Apostle Paul who wrote, *Since we have the same spirit of faith according to what has been written, 'I believed, and so I spoke,' we also believe, and so we also speak, knowing that he who raised the Lord Jesus will raise us also with Jesus and bring us with you into his presence. For it is all for your sake, so that as grace extends to more and more people it may increase thanksgiving to the glory of God (2 Corinthians 4:13-15).*

Biblical conviction, lived out, increases thanksgiving to God's glory.

That is why I include the information from William Bradford's journal as well as other historical gleanings. It is my desire that we see biblical conviction illustrated in history and that we therefore give thanks to God for His faithfulness.

William Bradford's objective in writing his journal is clear: *My object is that their children may see with what difficulties their fathers had to wrestle in accomplishing the first beginnings; and how God ultimately brought them through, notwithstanding all their weakness and infirmities; also that some use may be made of them later, by others, in similar important projects.*[8]

Bradford and the rest of the Pilgrims would rise up against us if we idealized them. They would also rebuke us, I think, if we seek to make their story unique in the annals of history to the neglect of God's providential work throughout the rest of history. However, Bradford wanted us to read, learn and remember the faith and fortitude of our forefathers. Upon the shoulders of such courageous Christians we stand.

I have chosen to rely upon Bradford because we so often associate our modern celebration of Thanksgiving Day with the Pilgrims of the 1600's and that first Thanksgiving in 1621. However, thanksgiving is not captive to any particular period of history. The Bible teaches that Christians are to be people of thanksgiving. Don't get lost in the illustrations and application seen in the Pilgrim fathers and mothers. Don't get sidetracked by the Presidential proclamations or the perseverance of Sarah Hale. Go back to the foundation—the Bible—and learn the priority of giving thanks to God.

When leading family worship make sure that it is abundantly clear in your statements and in your example that the Bible is the standard of faith and practice. Read the passages associated with each day. The readings will likely stir up your memory of other related texts. Turn to those as well. My primary objective in writing this book is not that you will know more about the Pilgrims, more about Thanksgiving proclamations and the first Thanksgiving Day. It is not that you will be a better student of American history. If any of those things result, remember they are good and helpful, but only side benefits. The objective is that you will know, worship and give thanks to God with your family.

Family worship is not about worshiping the family nor is it about worshiping the great heroes of the past. It is about leading one's family to worship God. God is revealed sufficiently and savingly in the Bible. Therefore, emphasize that which God has promised to bless in the salvation and sanctification of his people.

Begin · family worship with Scripture reading, follow with prayer, and continue with explanation and then close with application and prayer. The season of Thanksgiving is also an opportunity to become acquainted or reacquainted with some of the great hymns of Thanksgiving. You will find some of those hymns listed near the end of this book.

Introductory Thoughts

This is the third book in my series on family worship. The subject of family worship is exciting to me for several reasons:

1. God is to be worshiped. God is passionate about worship and therefore worship must be the priority of His people.
2. I love my family. I believe every day that I am falling short of God's glory in all sorts of ways. I am especially convicted that I need to be more faithful in leading my family to worship God. My desire is that we as a family make God's priority our own.
3. I have a vision for the future. For much of my Christian life I did not think much in terms of "the generations to come" (Psalm 78). When I first became a Christian I read the Bible diligently but my application was primarily personal. I thought little of my responsibility to the larger body of Christ. In recent years my thinking has been challenged by passages like Psalm 78, Psalm 127, Deuteronomy 6, Romans 15 and others. Reading those texts has been like an alarm clock going off in my soul. Wake up and look back to the faithfulness of God in history, engage the present generation with His Word and reach forward to the next generation. Multigenerational thinking was new for me, though the Bible is constantly

calling us to such thinking. This has enlarged my vision and has become an essential part of my writing and teaching ministry. The vision is that God would be glorified as we remember His faithfulness and as we promote his glory to future generations.

With my excitement about family worship I have also come to recognize some potential dangers:

1. The danger of not leading one's family to worship God. I can almost hear the voices of some of the Puritan pastors railing against those who failed to lead their families in worship. "Don't you care about the eternal destiny of your children? Will you not lift a finger to help your children avoid hell and receive heaven?" Those are some of the soul penetrating questions that the Puritans would ask. However, they couched their rebukes in lovely words of vision. They portrayed the home as a little church where God was to be worshipped.

2. The danger of placing too much emphasis on family.

John Wesley is not necessarily the model for being an excellent family man. However, he hits the mark with this statement:

Let this be carefully considered, even by those whom God has joined together; by husbands and wives, parents and children. It cannot be denied, that these ought to love one another tenderly. They are commanded to do so. But they are neither commanded nor permitted to love one another idolatrously. Yet how common is this: How frequently is a husband, a wife, a child put in the place of God. How many there are accounted good Christians who fix their affection on each other, so as to leave no place for God; They seek their happiness in the creature not the creator...Now if this is

not flat idolatry, I cannot tell what is." (unknown source of
Wesley's quote).

It is possible for one's spouse or children to be so neglected
that God is dishonored as the normal and tender bonds of
affection are loosened. It is also possible for one's spouse or
children to be so emphasized that they are enthroned and
elevated beyond what is proper. This is a more subtle
temptation. Such a sin will eventually manifest itself in other
sins such as a wrong view of the church.

Congregational life may sometimes be deemphasized all in the
name of the well being of the family. Godly churches that are
not "family friendly" enough in the estimation of a family
idolater will be abandoned in search of another church that will
better bow down to the idol of family. There may be some
parents who choose not to attend congregational gatherings at
all but instead opt for private family worship (with perhaps a
few friends). That thinking needs to be challenged as God has
called His people to gather together (Hebrews 10:24-25). That
being said there does seem to be far too much segregation of
the family in many otherwise doctrinally sound churches.

Let us properly love, regard and show affection to our family.
Let us sacrifice for their well-being and seek to protect them
from danger. Let us lead them to the well of Scripture and
encourage them to linger long and drink much. However, if
we worship them then we will be working towards their
destruction. God alone is to be worshiped. It is only when we
love God best that we can love our families as we should.

DAY ONE

Scripture Reading: Hebrews 11:13

Hebrews 11 has been called the "Hall of Fame of Faith." This passage gives a sweeping tour of some of the faithful men and women of biblical history. Many are named such as Abel, Abraham and even Rahab the prostitute. Others are simply referred to as those who *"...suffered mocking and flogging and even chains and imprisonment"* (36). All of those listed in Hebrews 11 were faithful. Why do you think God would list Rahab in the "Hall of Fame of Faith?"

Historical Glimpse

One hundred and twenty people met together in Southampton, England to board the *Mayflower*. That meeting was preceded by a small group of pilgrims (forty six) leaving Delftshaven, Holland (June 22, 1620). This group would meet up with the rest at Southampton to begin the long journey to the New World. Dr. Paul Jehle gives a summary of that meeting and then recounts Williams Bradford's description of the embarkation from Holland:

"... several families would be leaving behind wives and children, and even their Pastor, John Robinson, would be staying behind to tend to the majority of the members of the church who could not at this time make such a voyage. Bradford describes the departure from Delftshaven and it is from his comment that the 'Separatists' became known as 'Pilgrims' (taken from Hebrews 11:13 of the Bible)."[9]

So being ready to depart, they had a day of solemn humiliation...pouring out prayers to the Lord with great fervency, mixed with abundance of tears. And the time being come that they must depart, they were accompanied with most of their brethren out of the city, unto a town sundry miles off called Delftshaven, where the ship lay ready to receive them. So they left that goodly and pleasant city which had been their resting place near twelve years, but they knew they were pilgrims, and looked not much on those things, but lifted up their eyes to the heavens, their dearest country, and quieted their spirits.[10]

Theological Thought

Thanksgiving requires faith. Challenges to our faith, sickness in our body and trials of every sort can tend to overwhelm us. In our fallen world suffering abounds. However, our hope is not trapped by present circumstances. Christians are and have always been a pilgrim people looking to the future. As we look forward we must acknowledge that we are "strangers and exiles on the earth."

DAY TWO

Scripture Reading: I Chronicles 16:8

Our passage today reminds us that thanksgiving is to be directed to God. After all He is the ultimate source of every blessing and He is the one that is working all things for the good of His people (Romans 8:28). So though we are thankful for and to our family, friends and others let us never forget that it is the Lord who is our God!

Historical Glimpse

William Bennett writes, *Our first Thanksgiving was, of course, held by the Pilgrims in the fall of 1621. Washington's Thanksgiving Proclamation was our first national Thanksgiving. Abraham Lincoln in 1863 made it an annual national holiday to be celebrated on the last Thursday of November. Originally, it was a day of thanks and prayer and supplication and request for divine blessing. A few helpings of those would go nicely and wouldn't hurt with the stuffing and gravy of today.* [11]

It is fitting that our first President led the nation in its first national Thanksgiving celebration. When George Washington died Congress adopted the eulogy written by Henry "Light-Horse Harry" Lee as a part of the official record. Lee wrote of Washington, "First in war, first in peace, first in the heart of his countrymen."

Washington was first in many respects. His Thanksgiving Proclamation is invaluable. It reads...*Whereas it is the duty of all Nations to acknowledge the providence of Almighty God, to obey his will, to be grateful for his benefits, and humbly to implore his protection and favor, and Whereas both Houses of Congress have by their joint Committee requested me 'to recommend to the People of the United States a day of public thanks-giving and prayer to be observed by acknowledging with grateful hearts the many signal favors of Almighty God, especially by affording them an opportunity peaceably to establish a form of government for their safety and happiness...*

Theological Thought

Washington acknowledged that that it is "the duty of all Nations to acknowledge the providence of Almighty God..." Thanksgiving, though often forgotten, is nevertheless a duty. Scripture commands the people of God to be thankful. The command serves as a wake-up call. It is to God that we are to be thankful and it is God that we are to obey. Every time that we pray we should ...*not be anxious about anything, but in everything by prayer and supplication with thanksgiving let your requests be made known to God. And the peace of God which surpasses all understanding, will guard your hearts and your minds through Christ Jesus* (Philippians 4:6-7). It is true that thanksgiving is to be from the heart. However, the duty helps to stir the affections and affections help to fuel the duty. Take note of some of the commands to thanksgiving in the Bible such as Psalm 50:14. A concordance will help you. Perhaps it goes against the grain of your thinking that thanksgiving is a command. Why do you think that is the case?

DAY THREE

Scripture Reading: Ephesians 1:16

Do you give thanks to God for his people? One of the marks of a true Christian is love for other Christians (see I John 4:7-12). A Christian is one who is indwelt by the Holy Spirit. A primary result of the ministry of the Spirit is love (Galatians 5:22). The Christian is learning to love even his enemies and he has a growing and unique love for fellow believers. Is that true of you? It is a good and convicting question. One of the challenges in relationships is learning to value one another in spite of differences. Christians share a "like faith" but in other ways they are very unique. God has created us with multi-faceted gifts, talents and personalities. Have you learned the grace to appreciate the God-given variety in your fellow Christians? Have you learned to say, based on your faith in Jesus Christ, *I do not cease to give thanks for you, remembering you in my prayers* (Ephesians 1:16)?

These words from a beautiful Christian song serve to illustrate this vital truth –

27

Beneath the cross of Jesus
His family is my own—
Once strangers chasing selfish dreams,
Now one through grace alone.

How could I now dishonor
The ones that you have loved?
Beneath the cross of Jesus
See the children called by God.[12]
(Song: "Beneath the Cross of Jesus" by Keith and Kristyn Getty)

Historical Glimpse

The "historical glimpse" today reaches into the days of the early church. The impact of the early church on the unbelieving world around them was primarily a result of their unselfish love for one another. Such love is seen also in Acts 2:42-47.

John MacArthur in his commentary on Acts records an apology (defense) written by the philosopher Aristides early in the second century:

Now the Christians, O King, by going about and seeking, have found the truth. For they know and trust in God, the Maker of heaven and earth, who has no fellow. From him they received those commandments which they have engraved on their minds, and which they observe in the hope and expectation of the world to come.

For this reason they do not commit adultery or immorality; they do not bear false witness, or embezzle, nor do they covet what is not theirs. They honor father and mother, and do good to those who are their neighbors. Whenever they are judges, they judge uprightly. They do not worship idols made in the image of man. Whatever they do not wish that others should do to them, they in turn do not do; and they do not eat the food sacrificed to idols.

Those who oppress them they exhort and make them their friends. They do good to their enemies. Their wives, O King, are pure as virgins and their daughters are modest. Their men abstain from all unlawful sexual conduct and from iniquity, in the hope of recompense that is to come in another world.

As for their bondmen and bondwomen, and their children, if there are any, they persuade them to become Christians; and when they have done so, they call them brethren without distinction.

They love one another; the widow's needs are not ignored, and they rescue the orphan from the person who does him violence. He who has gives to him who has not, ungrudgingly and without boasting. When the Christians find a stranger, they bring him to their homes and rejoice over him as a true brother. They do not call brothers those who are bound by blood ties alone, but those who are brethren after the Spirit and in God.

When one of their own passes away from the world, each provides for his burial according to his ability. If they hear of any of their number who are imprisoned or oppressed for the name of the Messiah, they all provide for his needs, and if it is possible to redeem him, they set him free.

If they find poverty in their midst, and they do not have spare food, they fast two or three days in order that the needy might be supplied with the necessities. They observe scrupulously the commandments of their Messiah, living honestly and soberly as the Lord their God ordered them. Every morning and every hour they praise and thank God for his goodness to them; and for their food and drink they offer thanksgiving...[13]

Theological Thought

God's love in the hearts of His people is an uncontainable love. It is a love that must flow from the heart. It would be un-Christian to attempt to squelch the unquenchable love of God. *But if anyone has the world's goods and sees his brother in need, yet closes his heart against him, how does God's love abide in him (I John 3:17).* How is it possible to say that God's love abides in a person that does not express that love towards others? When John refers to seeing a brother in need that is a sure indication that we should be aware, sensitive and have our eyes open to the needs of our fellow Christians. Seeing a need, having some way to meet the need, a true Christian cannot contain love. Love must be expressed. Thanksgiving is the same way. The very nature of thanksgiving is expressive.

DAY FOUR

Scripture Reading: Romans 8:28-30

The providence of God refers to his governance of the universe. In the providence of God all things work for the good of Christians unto the glory of God. The word "accident" has no place in the vocabulary of the godly. The hand of Providence is guiding all of the details of the universe and of our lives. According to the Bible, God is bringing all things towards His designed purposes. This great truth should bring comfort and thanksgiving to the Christian.

Historical Glimpse

Horton Davies writes of the Puritan's view of God's providence in all things. *The chief occasions for New England thanksgivings were three: harvests saved in the early years of the settlements, the arrival of ships when famine was predicted, or the arrival of friends...The first Thanksgiving Day in New England was held in the fall of 1621, as recorded by William Bradford's* Of Plymouth Plantation, *although the exact day is not listed. It was in gratitude for the very first harvest of the Pilgrims. It was an extended celebration lasting three days. However, the first generally celebrated Day of Thanksgiving in New England was held in 1637 on October 12. This celebrated the victory of the colonial soldiers over the Pequot Indians.*

Davies notes that in times of greater difficulty the Puritans called for more days of Thanksgiving. *He says, "...This argues that the New England Puritans were grateful that matters were not as bad as they feared."[14]*

Theological Thought

Are you growing in your understanding that for the Christian all things work together for good? That does not mean that everything is good but that God is superintending all things. Understanding this gives the freedom to give thanks in all things. The providence of God is a comfort to His people. Even when things are bad we can be thankful that they are not worse. Challenging times remind us of the awfulness of sin, our need for Christ and the sweetness of heaven.

DAY FIVE

Scripture Reading: Philippians 4:11

Would you say that you are a content person? The Apostle Paul had suffered much. He had been imprisoned, beaten multiple times, stoned, shipwrecked, and faced a variety of dangers as well as times of hunger and thirst. He also was burdened with many pressures due to his care for the churches (2 Corinthians 11:16-28). All of that being true Paul was able to say, *...for I have learned in whatever situation I am to be content. I know how to be brought low, and I know how to abound. In any and every circumstance, I have learned the secret of facing plenty and hunger and abundance and need. I can do all things through him who strengthens me* (Philippians 4:11-13).

Historical Glimpse

Jeremiah Burroughs (1599-1646) was a faithful preacher of the gospel and prolific writer. He suffered much in ministry. He wrote the treasured book, *The Rare Jewel of Christian Contentment.* One of the chapters is titled, "Aggravations of the Sin of Murmuring." In the first heading of this chapter Burroughs writes, *To murmur when we enjoy an abundance of mercy; the greater and more abundant the*

mercy that we enjoy, the greater and viler is the sin of murmuring.
Burroughs encourages the reader to call to mind the great
mercies of God and weigh those mercies beside one's
sufferings. He then offers an objection and an answer:

Objection: "You will say, yes, but you do not know what
our afflictions are; our afflictions are such as you do not
conceive of because you do not feel them."

Answer: "Though I cannot know what your afflictions are,
yet I know what your mercies are, and I know they are so
great that I am sure there can be no afflictions in this
world as great as the mercies that you have. If it were
only this mercy that you have this day of grace and
salvation continued to you: it is a greater mercy than any
affliction. That you have the grace and salvation that you
are not now in hell, this is a greater mercy. That you have
the sound of the Gospel still in your ears, that you have
the use of your reason: this is a greater mercy than your
afflictions..." Burroughs continues on with this biblical
line of reasoning. Some of the passages that he uses to
illustrate his argument include: Numbers 16:8ff, Job 2:10,
Ecclesiastes 7:14.[15]

Burroughs did not write from a "flowery bed of ease" but
ministered under the weight of suffering. Get to know
this faithful Christian from history. You can learn much
about contentment and thanksgiving from him.

Theological Thought

Giving thanks to God is not dependent on one's personal
comfort and earthly satisfaction. Just as Paul stated that

he had learned to be content in both times of plenty and times of poverty, he also had learned to be thankful. A person who has found his contentment in Christ will necessarily be a thankful person. When Paul says, "I can do all things through him who strengthens me" he is saying that He can do all things with contentment through Christ. He was not saying that he had the ability to leap to the moon or run a two-minute mile. Paul was confident that regardless of his circumstances that he could be content—because of Jesus. Since that was true of Paul, it should be true of you.

DAY SIX

Scripture Reading: Psalm 100

When Christians consider the theme of thanksgiving, Psalm 100 races to their minds. The passage calls upon the faithful to *enter His gates with thanksgiving, and his courts with praise! Give thanks to him; bless his name! For the LORD is good; his steadfast love endures forever; and his faithfulness to all generations* (Vs. 3-4). The context of Psalm 100 refers to congregational worship. The Psalmist says, "Enter his gates with thanksgiving..." The worshiper of God should come to congregational worship with a heart of thanksgiving.

Historical Glimpse

Charles Haddon Spurgeon has often been referred to as, "The Prince of Preachers." He was a faithful preacher and a voluminous writer. The most exhaustive collection of Spurgeon's writings is found in *The Metropolitan Tabernacle Pulpit."* Perhaps his best exegetical and expository work is *The Treasury of David.* There, Spurgeon gives masterful expositions of the Psalms and includes a number of helps for preachers. In his comments from Psalm 100 he writes:

...It is all ablaze with grateful adoration, and has for this reason been a great favorite with the people of God ever since it was written. 'Let us sing the Old Hundredth' is one of the everyday expressions of the Christian church, and will be so while men exist whose hearts are loyal to the Great King. Nothing can be more sublime this side of heaven than the singing of this noble Psalm by a vast congregation. In this divine lyric we sing with gladness the creating power and goodness of the Lord, even as before with trembling we adored his holiness.[16]

If you do not own *The Treasury of David* then this would be a great set for you to purchase for your library at home or church. Spurgeon is one of the greatest preachers, pastors and writers in Christian history.

Theological Thought

Charles Spurgeon wrote, *In all our public service the rendering of thanks must abound. So long as we are receivers of mercy we must be givers of thanks. Mercy permits us to enter his gates; let us praise that mercy. What better subject for our thoughts in God's own house than the Lord of the house.*[17] When a Christian congregation gathers, thanksgiving must be scattered throughout the gathering. Such a worship service is honoring to the One to whom we owe thanks.

DAY SEVEN

Scripture Reading: Psalm 118:1; Titus 3:4-7

The goodness of God is evident to those who will take time to see! Acts 14:17 teaches that the goodness of God has always been on display as a witness to His character: *Yet he did not leave himself without witness, for he did good by giving you rains from heaven and fruitful seasons, satisfying your hearts with food and gladness."* The greatest display of the goodness of God is in the sending of His Son Jesus to die for sinners.

Historical Glimpse

George Washington spoke of the "duty of all nations to acknowledge the Providence of Almighty God." A presidential proclamation is in essence an advisement. It is not law but reflects a recommendation from the Commander in Chief. Even though President Lincoln's proclamation of 1863 began a string of such proclamations that continues today, his proclamation was not binding. Sarah Hale sought a more binding declaration from Congress. She wanted the fourth Thursday in November to be established as a federal holiday. She used Washington's proclamation to argue her point because he said that it was a nation's duty to "acknowledge the providence of God." Finally in 1941 (long after Sarah Hale had died) the 77th Congress established officially, that the last Thursday of November would be the legal, federally mandated holiday. However, the first draft had to be amended because they initially established the last Thursday as the official holiday and it was determined that Thanksgiving should be the fourth Thursday.

Joint Resolution

Making the last Thursday in November a legal holiday.

Resolved by the Senate and the House of Representatives Of the United States of America in Congress assembled, That the last Thursday of November in each year after the Year 1941 be known as Thanksgiving Day, and is hereby Made a legal public holiday to all intents and purposes and In the same manner as the 1ˢᵗ day of January, the 22ⁿᵈ day of February, the 30ᵗʰ day of May, the 4ᵗʰ day of July, the First Monday of September, the 11ᵗʰ day of November, and Christmas Day is now made by law public holidays.

Passed the House of Representatives October 6, 1941.

The Senate amended this on December 9, 1941 to read the "fourth" instead of the last Thursday of November.[18]

Sarah Hale is much to be credited for her work in both the Presidential proclamations from Lincoln onward. She planted the seed that resulted in the Congressional resolution of 1941.

Theological Thought

It is indeed the duty of nations and individuals to give thanks to God. The Bible commands thanksgiving. *But we ought always to give thanks to God for you, brothers beloved by the Lord, because God chose you..." (2 Thessalonians 2:13* emp. added*).* The Bible refers to giving thanks as the *will of God* (I Thessalonians 5:18). When civil authorities issue laws it is our duty to obey them unless those laws violate the law of God (Romans 13). However, even without a legal day of Thanksgiving, Christians are required to give thanks and in fact will desire to give thanks to God.

It is not a matter of spirituality whether one celebrates a national holiday or not. *Therefore, let no one pass judgment on you in questions of food and drink, or with regard to a festival or a new moon or a Sabbath. These are a shadow of the things to come, but the substance belongs to Christ (Colossians 2:16-17).*

It is permissible for a Christian to choose not to participate in national or religious festivals. Participating or not participating isn't a test of fellowship or of spiritual maturity. The same is true concerning eating and drinking. Christians have much freedom in what they eat, drink and how or if they celebrate special days. That freedom is not to be used for sinful purposes or with insensitivity towards the body of Christ—but it is a freedom nonetheless. We should be careful not to judge a person by standards that are not clearly defined in the Bible.

Regardless of whether or not you celebrate Thanksgiving Day, it is the solemn and joyful duty of all Christians to give thanks. It's a matter of the heart bathed in awareness of how kind God has been through sending His Son—not a matter of any particular day.

DAY EIGHT

Scripture Reading: 2 Corinthians 1:3-7

Of all of the writings of Paul, perhaps 2 Corinthians is the letter that focuses most on the theme of comfort. In fact the Greek words for comfort in 2 Corinthians are found there more than in any other New Testament book. Suffering is a fact of life in our fallen world. Everyone suffers on some level and for most of us significant suffering is just around the corner. Someone you know will get ill or die. A family that you are close to may break up. One of your children may rebel. You may lose your savings. You may find yourself rejected for taking a stand for Jesus. Though suffering is in your future you are not to be gripped by fear. Thank God for His present mercies and trust Him for the future. Though the focus of our passage today is suffering for the sake of the gospel, the language used encompasses any suffering that we face. God is the God of *all* comfort. He comforts us in "all of our affliction." The good news is that in our suffering we can know the comfort of God. His comfort is a concrete comfort that enables us to face our difficulties with faith and thanksgiving. You might say it is an active comfort. When a Christian suffers then God sends His comfort to aid the Christian in his struggle. Let us give thanks to our great God.

Historical Glimpse

The origins of Thanksgiving Day in America began on the shores of England by godly people who found themselves the target of attack by both church and state. In William Bradford's journal he cites, *suppression of religious liberty in England as the first cause of the foundation of the New Plymouth Settlement.*"[19]

Under Queen Mary many faithful Christians were martyred and many others fled the country. Among Christians that fled, disputes arose between those favoring a more ritualistic form of Christianity and those who wanted a more apostolic and simple biblical practice of worship. The second group was called Dissenters.

When Queen Elizabeth came to the throne some were hopeful that religious reform in a true biblical manner would ensue. They were mostly disappointed. She gave offices to some of those who fled under Mary but who were nonetheless Episcopal in their view of church life. Those state church adherents—many of them—grew in their disdain for the Dissenters. The Dissenters were called Puritans, a term originally of derision. Great suffering followed. We will do a brief sketch of these Dissenters' journey to America and the first formal Thanksgiving Day in studies to come. Suffice for now to remember that being a thankful person is not dependent on external circumstances. The Dissenters illustrated that truth by their teaching, convictions, courage and thanksgiving.

Theological Thought

Most of us tend not to think much about suffering and when we do, we are filled with many questions about God and why we suffer. Though all suffering in a general sense is due to sin, not all suffering is necessarily due to some specific sin (see John 9:1-7 and Job 1). In fact the Bible teaches that godliness results in suffering. Sometimes a person suffers because of a specific sin. Sometimes they suffer because they are being faithful to Christ. All suffering is a result of sin and the fall. To be faithful in the midst of suffering is to be careful not to waste your suffering. Suffering provides an opportunity to repent of sin, receive God's comfort, comfort others and worship God. Think about it.

DAY NINE

Scripture Reading: 2 Corinthians 1:11

Did you know that when you are faithful in prayer, others are motivated to give thanks to God? God's children are often afflicted. Sometimes the affliction is a gospel affliction. Trouble is the companion of the one who lives a godly life (2 Corinthians 1:8-9). Paul certainly knew about such tribulation (2 Corinthians 6:4-5). In our reading for today it is clear that when God blesses His people through prayer then "many will give thanks." Are you inspiring thanksgiving in others via your devotion in prayer?

Historical Glimpse

William Bradford described the church in his day as *hunted and persecuted.* "Some were clapped into prison; others had their houses watched night and day, and escaped with difficulty; and most were obliged to fly, and leave their homes and means of livelihood. Yet these and many other severer trials, which afterwards befell them, being only what they expected, they were able to bear by the assistance of God's grace and Spirit."[20]

It is interesting that these Christians were faithful to their duties in the midst of great suffering. Prior to their decision to journey to Holland where they expected greater religious freedom, Bradford writes: *So after about a year, having kept their meeting for the worship of God every Sabbath in one place or another, notwithstanding the diligence and malice of their adversaries, seeing that they could no longer continue under such circumstances, they resolved to get over to Holland as soon as they could—which was in the years 1607 and 1608.*[21]

The Christian's responsibility to worship God through congregational gathering is not an option but a joyful and necessary duty. A key ingredient in those gatherings is faithful prayer and thanksgiving.

Theological Thought

The sort of prayer that inspires thanksgiving grows out of these convictions:

1. Prayer helps. Paul says, "You must help us by prayer." When you pray for a fellow Christian you are helping them.
2. God uses the prayers of His people to bless those being prayed for. This is another way of stating point one. It is obvious from the text that we have a responsibility to pray and that God is willing and desires to answer prayer.

God chooses to help Christians who suffer "any affliction" by providing comfort that comes as a result of prayer.

Never think for a moment that prayer is a trivial thing. Prayer moves the hand of God.

DAY TEN

Scripture Reading: 2 Corinthians 1:1-11

This text reminds us of how we are to respond to "our affliction" as we share in "Christ's sufferings." There are many questions that we might have when we suffer. Sometimes we wonder why we suffer? The better question may be in relation to why God gives us seasons of comfort. There are many things to consider when thinking about and going through hardship. It is essential that we develop a biblical/theological framework for understanding and dealing with suffering.

Historical Glimpse

The sufferings that William Bradford and all of the Pilgrims faced were many and varied. As we have learned, many Christians fled the persecution of Queen Mary. Eventually some would flee to Holland. Bradford writes, "For those reformers to be thus constrained to leave their native soil, their land and livings and all their friends was a great sacrifice and wondered at by many. They went to an unknown country, language and their livelihood was in doubt. But these things did not dismay them for their desires were set on the ways of God, to enjoy His ordinances: they rested on His providence and knew whom they had believed."[22]

These Christians had more than a little difficulty getting to Holland. They faced hindrances of all sorts. They were robbed and even separated from their spouses for an extended time. When we think of the roots of our national Thanksgiving Day we must remember that those roots are planted in the soil of suffering and watered with the tears of broken hearts. However, the Pilgrims were motivated to give thanks to God for His great care over them.

The Pilgrims faced many dangers at sea on their journey to Holland and later to New England. At one point it is recorded that the seamen cried, "We sink, we sink." The Pilgrims responded, "Yet Lord Thou canst save."

Theological Thought

Our text today teaches us a number of things about suffering:

1. God is to be praised because He is the *Father of mercies and God of all comfort who comforts us in all our affliction*...(3-4).
2. Suffering gives us opportunity to be unselfish. God comforts us ...*so that we may be able to comfort those who are in any affliction, with the comfort with which we ourselves are comforted by God* (4). In other words when we suffer we are to be a conduit of blessing and comfort to others.
3. Suffering reminds us that we *share abundantly in Christ's sufferings so that through Christ we may share*

abundantly in comfort too (5). Our Lord is a sympathetic Savior (Hebrews 4:14-16). He suffered on our behalf and set an example for us on how to suffer. We are identified with our Savior when we have faith in God as we suffer (I Peter 4:12-19).

4. Suffering identifies us with other believers. We are not alone in our suffering but are members of a large family of fellow sufferers (6-7).
5. Suffering reminds us that the anchor holds. We are often tempted to rely on people or things. Suffering has a way of unloosening our grip on uncertain things so that we might better learn to rely on God (9). God who raises the dead comes to our aid as we suffer. Set your hope on Him (10).
6. Suffering summons the people of God to cry out in prayer and to remember that God blesses His people (11). This sort of prayer results in thanksgiving.
7. Some of the reasons that we suffer are so that we might know God's comfort, comfort others, and learn to trust in God (2 Corinthians 1:3-4, 9).

Personal note

Our family has been working through the grief of losing a baby via miscarriage. Tears have been a regular visitor to our home. Paul's second letter to the Corinthians has been a help to us as we have been made more aware of God's comfort. We have received the comfort that God has given through the prayers of His people. We have also been reminded that we are in a large family of fellow sufferers. We are discovering in new ways that God is the "God of all comfort" who "comforts us in all our afflictions." Our theology of prayer is deepening as a result. The Lord providentially brought a book to our home that has also served to encourage us. The book is *Where is God in All of This* by Deborah Howard. The following quote has been very helpful:

> *Suffering brings us pain, tears and heartache. He gave us tear ducts for a reason. It is not wrong to grieve, or sinful to be sad. He has never commanded us to be unemotional, unfeeling robots. Yet through our tears, we can still raise our eyes to the Almighty. We can still keep a godly perspective through any trial. Don't think God is oblivious to our tears and our suffering.*[23]

Howard then quotes Charles Spurgeon:

> *When a tear is wept by you, think not your Father does not behold, for, 'Like as a father pitieth his children, so the Lord pitieth them that fear him.' Your sigh is able to move the heart of Jehovah, your whisper can incline His ear to you, your prayer can stay His hands, your faith can move His arm. Oh! Think not that God sits on high in an eternal slumber, taking no account of you.*[24]

DAY ELEVEN

Scripture Reading: Proverbs 22:3

Today's verse reads, *The prudent sees danger and hides himself, but the simple go on and suffer for it.* Christians are to use wisdom and forethought as they make plans for the future. It is not necessarily a demonstration of faith to remain in or walk into danger. In fact it can be foolish. There are times when, for the sake of the gospel, we must endure great hardship (2 Timothy 2:1-13). We must always be ready and willing to face trial. However, we should be thoughtful, prayerful and seek godly counsel before walking into or remaining in danger. There is a time to face the battle and there is a time for the Christian to "hide himself." Wisdom is required to know the difference.

Historical Glimpse

After the Pilgrims arrived in Holland they noticed that the land was filled with plenty. However, they personally suffered much poverty. While in Amsterdam a church dispute deepened that resulted in a split. William Brewster thought it best that his group should move to Leyden. The church was lead by Brewster and Robinson and they were able to welcome a number of fellow Pilgrims from England. After several years the magistrates said of them, "These English have lived among us these 12 years and yet we never had any suit or accusation against any of them."[25]

Eventually they considered leaving Holland. The hardships were many, and some returned to England with no one replacing those who left. It was thought that if there could be found a better and easier place of living it would attract many and remove this discouragement.[26]

The Pilgrims were concerned for the elderly among them and their challenges. They were also concerned about their children who were described as "so oppressed by labor they became decrepit in early youth…the vigor of nature being consumed in the very bud."[27]

It was not only the suffering that their children faced that burdened the Pilgrims. As the children got older they were increasingly exposed to wickedness. The Pilgrim community was concerned about the impact that worldly influences were having on their offspring.

Under the heavy burden of natural hardship, care for the many elderly in their congregation, oppressive physical labor, temptation of their children and the opportunity to advance the gospel to the remote areas of the world, the Pilgrims determined to leave Holland and go to America.

Theological Thought

The Bible teaches, *The fear of the LORD is the beginning of wisdom, and the knowledge of the Holy One is insight* (Proverbs 9:10). The

Bible also teaches, *Be not wise in your own eyes; fear the LORD, and turn from evil* (Proverbs 3:7).

Though Christians should be courageous in all situations they should use wisdom when facing danger. Learn the difference between presumption and faith.

The Pilgrims' decision to move to America was an exchanging of hardships. Their decision involved a number of considerations that we can learn from:

1. They considered their elderly members.
2. They considered the physical and spiritual well being of their children.
3. They considered the congregation as a whole. They thought that the move to America would encourage others to join them in the work of raising their families and worshiping God freely.
4. They considered the advancement of the gospel to the remote corners of the world. They were driven by a vision for the glory of God.

These are considerations that every godly church should make a matter of prayer when making decisions. How will this decision impact the youngest and oldest among us? How will the decision impact the overall well-being of the congregation? How will the decision impact the advancement of the gospel?

DAY TWELVE

Scripture Reading: Psalm 78:1-7; Deuteronomy 6:1-15; Joshua 4

Biblical truth is to be learned, remembered, loved and passed down to the next generation. Family worship is one way that we seek to ensure that the next generation will know of the faithfulness of God. As we remember the work of God in the past we are encouraged to move forward in faith. Part of remembering how God has provided in ages past is to remember the ways that He worked through His servants. How much do you know about the people that God used to establish, build and sustain the country in which you live?

Historical Glimpse

The Pilgrims decided to face inevitable hardships and go to the New World. America held great promise but also many challenges. After an in-depth analysis they came to the conviction that God would bless them in their endeavors. There were English people already living in Virginia. The Pilgrims determined to live near enough to them that they might be able to come to assistance as needed, but far enough away that they could rule themselves. They would live under the general government of Virginia and petition the king for freedom of religion. The king did not grant such freedom but there were indications that he would not interfere with their worship.[28] Many logistical challenges had to be met, but ultimately they struck a deal with the Virginia Company that would bring them to America. Two ships were prepared. A small ship named the *Speedwell* would help transport some of the people and supplies. This ship was to stay with the Pilgrims as a help to them in getting established in the New World. The larger ship that would transport them was named the *Mayflower*.

Though all was arranged, plans were made and the course considered, there were still many struggles that transpired before the people could leave on the first leg of their journey. Bradford recorded part of his vision in his journal. He writes, "My object is that their children may see with what difficulties their fathers had to wrestle in accomplishing the first beginnings; and how God ultimately brought them through, notwithstanding all their weakness and infirmities; also that some use may be made of them later, by others, in similar important projects."[29]

Theological Thought

Biblically driven theology creates forward-looking people. One of the troubling things about the nations of the world is the emphasis on present gratification. For example, nations burden themselves with almost unimaginable debt that is borrowed from future generations. Their thinking is built on the assumption (or presumption) that there will be money in the future to cover the debts of the present generation.

The Bible confronts such self-centered thinking and prods us to look ahead to our great-great grandchildren. That sort of vision requires us to look back to our first beginnings, and the difficulties of our forefathers, and the faithfulness of God. Understanding our beginnings will help us to properly convey the lessons of the past to those who will follow in our footsteps.

DAY THIRTEEN

Scripture Reading: Ezra 8:21

Our Scripture reading for today takes us back to the time of Ezra. He led the people to trust in God for the journey that was ahead of them. He did this by proclaiming a fast:

1. That the people might humble themselves before God.
2. To seek from God a safe journey "for ourselves, our children, and all our goods."

Historical Glimpse

As the Pilgrims prepared to depart Leyden where they had lived for nearly 12 years, their beloved pastor, John Robinson, led them to fast and pray. Pastor Robinson would be remaining for the time at Leyden to shepherd the flock that was staying behind. Many in the church could not yet embark upon the journey, needing more time to get their affairs in order and lacking enough room aboard ship. Robinson prayed that the door would one day be opened for them to join their brothers and sisters in New England. As they prepared to leave, many friends followed them to port. Tears from heavy hearts accompanied all. Even strangers watching from a distance were moved to tears. Mr. Robinson "fell down with the rest and with tears they prayed to God for His blessing."[30]

Theological Thought

I am writing this section on July 4[th.] Today was a day of rejoicing and giving thanks for the many liberties that we enjoy. These freedoms were paid for by the sacrifices of our forefathers and are maintained by those who are willing to defend them still today. That being said, there is an unhealthy independence that one might have. Being a Christian means that one has declared their dependence on God for salvation and sustenance. As our Scripture reading today reminded us, we are dependent upon God for a "safe journey" and we are dependent upon God for all things. That is why Ezra proclaimed a fast and led the people to pray. Prayer is declaring our dependence on God for help. When John Robinson knelt with the Pilgrims to pray, he was displaying that they were dependent upon God. In the early years of our country there were not only days of thanksgiving established but days of fasting and prayer. The Bible records times of feasting and times of deep brokenness, fasting and prayer. Read the books of Nehemiah and Ezra for examples of both.

DAY FOURTEEN

Scripture Reading: Hebrews 11:1-16

The life of faith requires us to move forward without all of the information. Read carefully so that you will not be misguided. Faith is not a blind leap into the dark. Faith, as has often been described, is a step into the light. The light is God's Word. There we find the scope of God's redemptive plan. However, the Bible does not give us the details of our daily lives. It does not tell us where to live, what to eat or how to find a job. It does give us wisdom for making such decisions. Faith requires that we trust in God by walking according to His Word. Hebrews 11 is a great chapter on such faith. Pilgrim people "acknowledge that they are strangers and exiles on the earth" (13).

Historical Glimpse

They knew they were pilgrims—William Bradford

As the Pilgrims prepared to leave Holland they fasted, prayed, and enjoyed lively fellowship with their friends. Once again they were pulling up roots in order to venture into new lands. Bradford writes "...but they knew they were pilgrims, and lifted up their eyes to the heavens, their dearest country, and quieted their spirits."[31]

When the Pilgrims arrived at Southampton the *Mayflower* was there to meet them along with those who would travel with them to New England. A letter from Mr. Robinson was read to the group. In this letter he expressed his love and assured them of his desire to join them as soon as possible. He challenged them to daily renew their repentance with our God. He then exhorted them to live in unity and peace with one another and others. He instructed them regarding civil government. He said,

...let your wisdom and godliness appear, not only in choosing such persons as will entirely love and promote the common good, but also in yielding them all due honor and obedience in their lawful administrations; not beholding in them the ordinariness of their persons, but God's ordinance for your good... But you know...and understand that the image of the Lord's power and authority, which the magistrate bears, is honorable, in how humble persons serve. And this duty you can the more willingly perform, because you are at present to have only those for your governors as you yourselves choose.[32]

His letter closes with a blessing and prayer.

These few things, therefore, I do earnestly commend unto your care and conscience, joining therefore, your daily incessant prayers unto the Lord, that He Who has made the heavens and the earth, the sea and all rivers of waters, and Whose providence is over all His works, especially over all His dear children for good, would so guide and guard you in your ways, as inwardly by His spirit, so outwardly by the hand of His power, that both you and we also may praise His name all the days of our lives. Fare you well in Him in Whom you trust, and in Whom I rest.[33]

Theological Thought

Bradford's words, "They knew they were pilgrims" raises an important point. Do you know that you are a pilgrim? Or do you find that your stakes are planted deep here on the earth?

Being a pilgrim does not necessarily mean that one is constantly moving from one location to another. It does mean that a person is willing at a moment's notice to make changes. The Christian understands that heaven is his eternal home and that this present life is temporary. Therefore he travels lightly and fixes his hope on Christ. The Christian pilgrim knows that God made all things and that He is superintending all that He has made. He is especially mindful of His children.

Day Fifteen

Scripture Reading: Proverbs 16:9

Planning is a good thing. However, it is essential to remember that all of our plans are dependent upon God. James writes: *Come now, you who say, 'Today or tomorrow we will go into such and such a town and spend a year there and trade and make a profit' Yet you do not know what tomorrow will bring. What is your life? For you are a mist that appears for a little time and then vanishes. Instead you ought to say, 'If the Lord wills, we will live and do this or that' (James 4:13-15)*. In a world of great confusion it is a comfort to know that God is directing our steps.

Historical Glimpse

The Pilgrims left Southampton with vision but plenty of uncertainty. However, they had faith in God. They made their plans. For many of them God would redirect their steps. They left on two ships, the *Mayflower* and the *Speedwell*. The *Speedwell* was the smaller ship and it began to take on too much water. Both ships docked for a time so that the small ship could be repaired. This was time consuming and expensive. After a while they left again and yet finally it was determined that the small ship would need to be sent back. They loaded as many supplies as they could aboard the *Mayflower* but had to send some supplies back and also some of their friends. Some of their friends volunteered to go back. This was another sad parting for people that had labored and suffered together. However, in the providence of God some were hindered from going to America and others went on to make the journey. The journey would not be filled with ease, like a relaxing voyage on a modern cruise ship. The trip was filled with many dangers and challenges. They were confident that God was directing their steps.

Theological Thought

The Bible is not opposed to long range planning. In fact, a careful reading of Proverbs will demonstrate that a wise man looks ahead and makes plans accordingly. However, the Christian is to make plans humbly, thoughtfully, prayerfully and under wise advisement. He should also make plans with a sense of great flexibility knowing that God may redirect his steps and change his plans. Whatever course God chooses for His people there is opportunity to worship God the way that Job did when God radically changed his life at the death of his ten children (Job 1:20-22).

Day Sixteen

Scripture Reading: Acts 27: 39-28:2

When Paul and the crew were shipwrecked they nevertheless faced a sweet providence from God. Paul said, *The native people showed us unusual kindness...* God was kind and would have been regardless of how Paul and his companions were greeted. It is our responsibility to acknowledge the providence and kindness of God whether our circumstances produce comfort or pain.

Historical Glimpse

It was September and the *Mayflower* was at sea. The ship and its passengers faced a number of frightening trials. There was even consideration of turning back out of fear that the ship could not complete the journey. However, the Pilgrims determined to continue on with faith in God. Bradford said "they committed themselves to the will of God."[34]

After a long beating at sea they finally saw the land called Cape Cod. They were filled with gladness. After more time of being in danger at sea and considering a landing near the Hudson River, they focused on Cape Cod. Bradford says that in sight of land they "fell on their knees and blessed the God of Heaven who had brought them over vast and furious ocean, and delivered them from all the perils and miseries of it, again to set their feet upon the firm and stable earth, their proper element."[35]

Bradford continues:

But here I cannot but make a pause, and stand half amazed at this poor people's present condition; and so I think will the reader, too when he considers it well. Having thus passed the vast ocean, and that sea of troubles before while they were making their preparations, they now had no friends to welcome them, nor inns to entertain and refresh their weather beaten bodies, nor houses—much less towns to repair to.[36]

Theological Thought

The Bible teaches that God cares for orphans and widows. Though we often may find ourselves without many of the comforts to which we have become accustomed, God is always very near. It is encouraging to be allowed the opportunity by the grace of our Savior to call God our Father. Let us give Him thanks. He is with us even when people and comforts are nowhere near.

DAY SEVENTEEN

Scripture Reading: I Corinthians 14:40; Romans 13:1-14

The Corinthians passage has reference to the public meetings of the church. Church services are to be biblical and orderly. Though the primary reference is to the church it is true that all things in life should be done in an orderly manner. That is true concerning how a people are governed. Romans chapter 13 gives more specific teaching on one's responsibility to government. Any government brings a degree of order to a society. Such order would not exist if everyone simply did what seemed right to him or her. It is good for us to meditate often upon our responsibilities to be ordered people in all respects, including our interaction with the governing authorities.

Historical Glimpse

Before the Pilgrims came ashore they developed a compact, or covenant, that came to be known as The Mayflower Compact. This compact illustrated their desire to be orderly, submissive to authority and to live their lives in community for God's glory. It reads,

In the name of God, Amen.

We whose names are underwritten, loyal subjects of our dread sovereign lord, King James, by Grace of God...and so forth, having undertaken, for the Glory of God and advancement of the Christian Faith, and honor of our King and Country, a voyage to plant the first colony in the northern parts of Virginia, do by this document solemnly and mutually in the presence of God, and one another, covenant and combine ourselves together into a civil body politic, for our bettering, ordering and preservation and furtherance of the ends aforesaid; and by virtue of this document enact, constitutions and offices, from time to time, as shall be thought right for the general good of the colony, unto which we promise all due submission and obedience. In witness we have hereunder subscribed our names at Cape Cod the eleventh of November, in the eighteenth year of the reign of our sovereign lord, King James. 1620 A.D.[37]

The first governor of the Pilgrims was Mr. John Carver. He and other leaders would later meet to discuss *laws and orders for their civil and military government as necessity required.*[38]

Theological Thought

Throughout church history Christians have compacted together as members of the church. The Church has a rich treasury of confessions, catechisms and creeds. Many churches today employ a constitution and bylaws to help their local church to be governed in accordance with Scripture. None of the documents mentioned above are to replace Scripture but should serve as a means to apply Scripture to congregational life.

Christians are to be disciplined (I Timothy 4:7) and should pray for an ordered and godly civil government (I

Timothy 2:1-7). There does not seem to be any directive in the New Testament for Christians to attempt to take over government. Christians are to submit to the governing authorities (except when doing so would violate God's law). Christians are also to pray for those in authority and to seek to live peaceably with all men. Believers in Christ are free to be involved in government and also to serve in the military. However, the focus of one's life is never an earthly kingdom, but rather the kingdom of heaven. Sometimes Christians get out of balance by too much focus on government and other times by being very passive towards government.

DAY EIGHTEEN

Scripture Reading: Psalm 30; Romans 8:28ff

Give thanks to the Lord. He is good. Recently a couple of friends were in a car accident. Of course we know that there is no such thing as an accident. God is in control even over "accidents." My friends were spared any injury. We rejoiced in the Lord. However, we are to learn to give thanks to the Lord regardless of the circumstances. The Lord is good even when "bad" things come into our lives. If we are His children then we can be confident that He works for our good and His glory even when we suffer.

Historical Glimpse

The Pilgrims arrived at Cape Cod on November 11, 1620. Soon after their arrival they sent out an exploration team. Insights about the Indians were revealed as the explorers found gravesites, buried corn and other traces of Indian culture. On their first exploration they saw a few Indians who ran from them. The explorers pursued in hopes of getting to know them but they could not find the Indians. On their third exploration the Indians attacked them. When they again pursued the Indians it was because they wanted to show that they were not afraid. No one was hurt. After many discoveries, numerous challenges and increasingly bad weather, they paused to thank God for His help. Bradford writes, "...they gave God solemn thanks and praise for their deliverance, and gathered up a bundle of the arrows." They called the place The First Encounter. Leaving to further explore the coastline, their boat became entangled in a storm and was weakened. Eventually by God's grace they made shore in an area unknown to them. They gave "God thanks for His mercies in their manifold deliverances." On December 15th they returned to this newly discovered place with the other Pilgrims and on December 25th they began to erect their first house for common use.[39]

Theological Thought

With the entrance of sin into the world came the entrance of chaos. The once beautiful Garden of Eden became ensnared with thorns. The once peaceful human community (initially consisting of two) began struggling in their relationship with one another. Murder soon followed, as did all sorts of sin (Genesis 4). All of creation was impacted (see Genesis 3 and Romans 5). This is why weeds strangle our gardens, city streets flow with blood, hurricanes devastate coastlines, and every other challenge confronts us. However, we must never think that chaos is ruling the day. God is sovereign. He was sovereign as the Pilgrims faced the struggles that they faced and He is sovereign now. Through Christ we find deliverance—not from all of the challenges of living in a fallen world but deliverance from ultimate harm befalling us. In fact, God is working good. What a cause for thanksgiving!

DAY NINETEEN

Scripture Reading: 2 Corinthians 4:7-18

Perhaps you may wonder why there would be such an emphasis on suffering in a book about thanksgiving. The Bible teaches that the Christian is to always give thanks to the Lord. Thanksgiving is even referred to as a sacrifice. Those who helped to lay the foundation of American society faced innumerable sufferings. Yet their example is one of thanksgiving. Though our bodies are frail and wasting away we are not to lose heart (16). We are to keep an eternal perspective.

Historical Glimpse

It is difficult to describe the suffering that the Pilgrims faced in their first few months of life in America. With the onslaught of winter and a variety of diseases afflicting the group, many grew ill, weak and faced death. Sometimes there was but a handful of people to care for the afflicted. Bradford notes that they were faithful in their care for one another. One of the men was William Brewster, their faithful pastor who nurtured the sick devotedly. By late February, it is likely that half of all who had made the journey had died. *Of one hundred people scarce fifty remained.*[40] It wasn't just the suffering of facing the elements and sickness. Numerous challenges met the Pilgrims as they sought to build their houses and establish their homes.

What if half of the people in your church were to die in the course of a couple of months? Imagine that 100 people attend your church on a regular basis and within three months only fifty remain. What kind of impact would that have upon the church, community and your family?

Nothing came easy for Bradford, Brewster and their fellow Pilgrims. They were seeking to build houses, a church building and a new life. We are surrounded by such conveniences that it is hard for us to conceive of a situation where there is not a store just around the corner. The character of the godly Pilgrims was tested in the furnace of suffering. We stand upon their strong shoulders. Never forget our history. Read *Of Plymouth Plantation* and communicate to your children the faithfulness of those sacrificial servants of Christ. Yes, indeed, our modern celebration of Thanksgiving is rooted in the soil of suffering saints who nevertheless knew what it was to give thanks to God.

Theological Thought

What is the worst thing that can happen to a person? During the 17th century in England and America the most recommended book other than the Bible was *A Token for Children* by James Janeway and Cotton Mather. In the introduction to a modern edition of the book

Henry Christoph writes: *Janeway's brief masterpiece is by no means all sad. The children whose lives are recounted all die, but that is not the worst thing that can happen to a child. Dying without Christ is the worst thing, which happens to none of the children in Janeway's book.*[41]

Though many of the Pilgrims died in the early days of their settlement, we have great confidence that they died in the Lord. Indeed the worst thing is not that a person dies. The worst thing is to die without Christ as Lord and Savior. The best thing is to know Christ and to live and be ready to die for His glory. Do you know Christ as your Lord? If not, repent and trust in the Savior who lived without sinning, died for sinners and was raised again from the dead.

DAY TWENTY

Scripture Reading: Nehemiah 8:10

Where does one find strength to endure the tremendous hardships that are the common lot of man? During the recent death of our unborn baby we received notes from around the nation. Many people opened their hearts to us and shared their testimonies of God's grace. One lady wrote of having multiple miscarriages at various stages in her pregnancies. Some of the miscarriages were very late term. We heard from a lady that shared the story of the birth of her baby—and the death of the baby three hours later. One mother told of the deaths of several children. How can one endure in a God-glorifying manner the sufferings of this life? Nehemiah reminds us that it is the joy of the Lord that is our strength.

Historical Glimpse

After the cold, hard and deadly days of winter the air began to warm and so did the hearts of the remaining Pilgrims. A friendly Indian that spoke broken English named Samoset came into their village. He had only been in the area for eight months. He told them much about the surrounding area. Indians had lived in the very area the Pilgrims now occupied but all that lived there had died of the plague. Samoset told them that they would not have to worry about Indians desiring to occupy the place again. They were superstitious about the ground and could not imagine living on the soil where so many had died. Samoset also told them of a man named Squanto that had been in England and spoke better English.

A few days later Samoset came again with five others, bearing items for trading. They seemed to be friendly, ate with the Pilgrims and sang and danced.

On the 22nd of March, Samoset returned bringing Squanto with him. The Indian leader Massosoit was nearby with 60 of his men. Edward Winslow was sent to meet with Massosoit and to seek peace and trade. The Pilgrims sent gifts.

Eventually a peace treaty was made with the Indians. "Squanto stayed with them and was their interpreter. He was a special instrument sent of God for their good... He showed them how to plant their corn, where to fish and get other things, and was also their pilot to bring them to unknown places for their profit, and never left them till he died."[42]

Theological Thought

Though God providentially allows trouble to afflict His dear children, He also brings sweet displays of His kindness to encourage them in their trials. God is for His people (Romans 8:31). He is actively working for their good. He hears their prayers and comes to their aid. If deep and painful suffering afflicts us, we should always remember that God is at work and will bring displays of His grace so that we might hold on in the midst of the storm.

One of the most encouraging stories in Christian history is of George Mueller. Mueller lived by faith in God's promises each day and by faith received all that he needed to provide for thousands of children, spread the gospel on missionary endeavors and care for his family. He did so without asking anyone other than God for help.

There have been many occasions in our family where we have not known how we were going to pay some expense. The funds were not readily available. We have sold items, worked multiple jobs and sought to be faithful. Time and again we have been recipients of the provision of God just when we have needed it. We have received items, financial assistance and the regular prayers of God's people. Even with the challenges that we as a family have faced, we have suffered nothing in comparison to what the Pilgrims endured. Regardless, the difficulties have provided new opportunity to trust God for help and thank Him for His loving care. Yes, challenges will come. However, for those who belong to Christ, God will meet every challenge with His generous provision of help.

DAY TWENTY-ONE

Scripture Reading: Psalm 147:7

One of the marks of true thanksgiving is that it is expressive. A thankful heart cannot long keep silent. It must express itself in song, testimony and proclamation. Have you been quiet too long? Sing thanksgiving to God.

Historical Glimpse

As the Pilgrims began to settle down in Plymouth they faced numerous challenges. Though springtime brought opportunity for fresh provision, they still faced struggles and relationship challenges with some of the Indians.

Squanto taught them how to plant corn and due to the wear and tear of the land pointed out the necessity of using fish in the soil as a means of fertilizing the crop. In the providence of God, Squanto continued to prove to be a help to the people.

Bradford gave God glory. "The spring now approaching, it pleased God the mortality began to cease among them, and the sick recovered apace, which put new life into them all; though they had borne their sad afflictions with as much patience and contentedness as I think any people could do. But it was the Lord who upheld them, and had beforehand prepared them, many having long borne the yoke, yea, even from their youth...March 25, 1621."[43]

Theological Thought

Think about the expressive nature of thanksgiving. A couple of examples in Scripture will suffice:

1. *Luke 17:11-17* Jesus healed ten lepers but only one returned to give thanks. All ten of the lepers had cried out for Jesus to help them. Jesus heard their cry and gave them instruction. He healed all ten of the lepers. However, only one expressed his thanksgiving to Jesus. *Then one of them, when he saw that he was healed, turned back, praising God with a loud voice, and he fell on his face at Jesus' feet giving him thanks. Now he was a Samaritan (Luke 17:1-16).* That is the sort of thanksgiving that Jesus expects. He expects that those whom he has helped will be thankful. In fact he asks three penetrating questions, *Were not ten cleansed? Where are the nine? Was no one found to return and give praise to God except this foreigner (17-18)?*

2. *Psalm 118:1-4* This passage opens with a call to give thanks to God. To "give thanks" denotes expression. In fact verse two declares, "Let Israel say..." Verse three opens with, "Let the house of Aaron say..." and verse four, "Let those who fear the LORD say..." To give thanks involves speaking. *Oh give thanks to the LORD; call upon His name; make known his deeds among the peoples! Sing to*

him, sing praises to him; tell of all his wondrous works" *(Psalm 105:1-2)*. The point is clear. Thanksgiving cannot be contained; it must be expressed.

Look up the references to thanksgiving in the Psalms and meditate on them. Sing the great hymn, *O for a Thousand Tongues to Sing* by Charles Wesley.

DAY TWENTY-TWO

Scripture Reading: James 2:14-17; I John 3:16-18

Unrealized expectations often result in disappointment. It is essential that we have a proper view of expectations. People cannot guarantee that they will be able to fulfill promises. Life is uncertain and all of our plans must be made humbly and with God's will in view. The promises of God are different. Whatever God promises is a divine certainty. Promises made by others are not as certain. That being said we must do all that we can to fulfill our promises to others beyond simply wishing them well.

For example we must do more than say to a hungry and needy person, "Be warmed and be filled." We must be moved to action. The Apostle Paul had a deep desire that Israel would be saved (Romans 10:1 -14). However he did not dream away with only wishful thinking. Paul activated his desires by prayer, preaching and perseverance. He worked for the salvation of his countrymen. Wishing another person well without a commitment to help them is useless to the person and dishonoring to God.

Historical Glimpse

The Pilgrims faced times of disappointment. Perhaps you can imagine them gazing out to the ocean and seeing a ship sailing towards them. They would have thought that perhaps some of their friends had finally been able to make the journey. They would have expected that the ship would bring to them fresh provision. However, they were often disappointed in that the ship brought more people but not more provision. Burdens were increased rather than relieved.

Promises had been made to the Pilgrims, but those promises had been broken. Expectations had been created, only to be dashed. People that had been trusted had shown themselves to be unworthy of that confidence.

Bradford is diligent in *Of Plymouth Plantation* to reflect on both the joys and the disappointments of the Pilgrims.

Theological Thought

A proper understanding of the Bible leads to the conclusion that God is sovereign over all things. When disappointment comes into our lives it brings with it a test to our reflexes. How will we respond?

Some become bitter, others cynical. There are those that simply become hopeless and throw caution to the wind or worse. Some choose the path of licentiousness (After all, what does it matter? Hopes and dreams have been dashed so often). Others choose despair and engage in destructive behavior.

The follower of Christ, however, has a higher calling. He is not a victim of the whims of people that disappoint or of dreams that fall short. He has rested his weight on One Who never disappoints. If the Lord gives or the Lord takes away, it is because the Lord knows what is most needful for His children at a particular time in their lives. He does not leave His beloved people to chance or circumstance; rather, He upholds them in His hand. Disappointments will come. The Christian, because of God's sovereignty and goodness can—and should—be thankful to God for His loving care.

DAY TWENTY-THREE

Scripture Reading: Psalm 100

You may want to adjust your readings to make this day your Thanksgiving Day devotion. Note: This is the second time we have used this Psalm. You may wish to choose another.

Paul indicates that contentment is something that the Christian learns as he grows in Christ (Philippians 4:11). During his ministry he had experienced times of great heights and deep, dark valleys. Even in his daily diet there were times of abundant provision and times when he suffered hunger. Through Christ he learned contentment.

The Pilgrims often found that they were in dire straits. In the fall of 1621, life had improved for a time—and comparatively speaking they had plenty. Their common song in good and bad times—was the song of thanksgiving.

Historical Glimpse

In the fall of 1621 the Pilgrims were more shielded from the weather and their farming efforts were productive. Bradford writes:

They began now to gather in the small harvest they had, and to prepare their houses for the winter, being well recovered in health and strength, and plentifully provisioned; for while some had been thus employed in affairs away from home, others were occupied in fishing for cod, bass and other fish, of which they caught a good quantity, every family having their portion. All the summer there was no want. And now, as winter approached, wild fowl began to arrive, of which there were plenty when they came here first, though afterwards they became more scarce. As well as wild fowl they got abundance of wild turkeys, besides venison, etc. Each person had about a peck of meal each week, or now, since harvest, Indian corn in that proportion; and afterwards many wrote at length about their plenty to their friends in England..."[44]

The book, *Pilgrim Courage* records,

The harvest gotten in, the Governor sent four men out fowling, so they could rejoice together after they had gathered the fruits of their labor. The four in one day killed enough fowl to feed the whole company a week with a few other things added. As a part of their recreations they had shooting matches. Many of the Indians came amongst them. They were entertained and feasted for three days. The Indians went out and killed five deer, which they brought to the plantation and gave to the Governor, the Captain, and others. And although it not always so plentiful as it was at this time, yet by the goodness of God the plantation was so far from want that they often wished those in England and Holland sharers of the plenty.[45]

Many people see the account above as the event which is most foundational in our celebration of Thanksgiving.

Theological Thought

The goodness of God should be celebrated. Bradford writes, *Thus out of small beginnings greater things have been produced by His hand that made all things out of nothing, and gives being to all things that are. As one small candle may light a thousand, so the light here kindled hath shone to many, yea in some sort to our whole nation. Let the glorious name of Jehovah have all the praise.*[46]

It is wise for the Christian to trace the hand of God's providence throughout history so that we might see how He has brought something from nothing. The result should be thanksgiving.

Day Twenty-Four

Scripture Reading: I John 3:11-4: 21

Biblical love reaches out to assist those in need. One of the tests as to the reality of a person's faith is their love for God and His people. Are you a loving person? That does not mean that you are simply polite and do no harm to others. Those things will be true of a loving person. However, biblically defined, love must reach out and assist those in need. This is how we know that we are His disciples.

Historical Glimpse

After that first Thanksgiving, and after the winter months that followed, there is recorded a remarkable providence of God.

Later in the spring one of the Indian leaders (Massasoit) that had become a great help to the Pilgrims became sick. The Pilgrims sent herbs and medicines to him. Massasoit appeared to be sick unto death. God preserved him and healed him at that time. This prompted Edward Winslow to say, 'We with admiration bless God for giving his blessing to such raw and ignorant means, making no doubt of his recovery, himself and all of them acknowledging us the instruments of his preservation. Never did I see a man so low brought, recover in that measure in so short a time.' A few days later Massasoit remarked, "Now I see the English are my friends and love me; and whilst I live, I will never forget this kindness they have showed me.[47]

Theological Thought

We have many opportunities to give testimony of God's love by showing love to others. This is to love as God loves. God has a unique, particular and specific love for His chosen children. However, He shows love towards all people in everything from a beautiful sunrise to the harvest of a garden. This is one way that God testifies of His glory (Acts 14:16-18). When a person rejects Christ they do so in the face of the evidence of His great love. This makes them guiltier. As Christians we must let our light of love shine so that even our enemies will know that we love them.

DAY TWENTY-FIVE

Scripture Reading: Acts 20:17-36

The Apostle Paul was a man of great strength because God granted him courage through his faith. Therefore God gets the glory for the courage of Paul. Paul knew that danger awaited him in Jerusalem but he was "constrained by the Spirit" and therefore he wrote: *"But I do not account my life of any value nor as precious to myself, if only I may finish my course and the ministry that I received from the Lord Jesus, to testify to the gospel of the grace of God."* Let us pray for the courage of our convictions and be focused on the gospel.

Historical Glimpse

Much of the historical information on previous pages has come from the journals of William Bradford—perhaps the best-known Pilgrim. Bradford was a man of deep conviction, courage and leadership ability. He suffered much on the journey to Plymouth and even lost his wife. He became very sick and at one point almost died due to a fire. He was an unselfish man. When reading *Of Plymouth Plantation*, it is easy to forget that Bradford himself is a part of the story that he is telling. He draws almost no attention to himself. Such was his humility. He was not on mission for self-centered objectives but wanted to serve God and his fellow man.

William Bradford was a man of great piety from the time of his youth. Many of his relatives mocked him for his identification with the Separatist movement. He confessed before his relatives at age 14:

...To keep a good conscience, and walk in such a way as God has prescribed in his word, is a thing, which I must prefer before you all, and above life itself. Wherefore, since 'tis for a good cause that I am like to suffer the disasters which you lay before me, you have no cause to be either angry with me; yea, I am not only willing to part with everything that is dear to me in this world for this cause, but I am also thankful that God has given me a heart to do, and will accept me so to suffer for him.[48]

Dr. Jehle writes,

As a teenager of barely sixteen, he joined the Separatist church that met in secret at Scrooby Manor, the home of William Brewster. At age eighteen, along with many of the other separatist Pilgrims, he was betrayed and put in jail in Boston, England for attempting to go to Holland. At age nineteen, he suffered near shipwreck on the voyage to Holland. Finally, along with the others, they did make it to Amsterdam for a year, and then to Leyden for eleven more years. Here he married Dorothy, and became a pillar in the church under the leadership of John Robinson. He came to the New World on the Mayflower after barely turning thirty, lost his wife who drowned in Provincetown harbor, and nearly lost his own life when the common house almost burned to the ground. He then found himself unanimously elected the second governor of Plymouth after the untimely death of the revered John Carver. Thus, in the spring of 1621, William Bradford began a career of leading the Plymouth colony almost without interruption until his death in 1657, at the age of sixty-seven.[49]

Theological Thought

The early days of American history are not foundational to our faith. However, they demonstrate an application of the truth. In William Bradford we find biblical conviction, a sensitive conscience, a willingness to suffer, a lack of love for the things of this world an unselfish spirit and a thankful heart.

Those are marks of devotion to Christ. Bradford was ridiculed by family and cast out. He suffered great loss and was imprisoned. He was compelled into significant leadership. Through it all he was thankful to God and served the Lord as a good soldier of Jesus Christ.

The life worth living is the one that is invested sacrificially in the well being of other people and in causes greater than oneself. The Apostle Paul was ready to live, ready to die—but either way he had a twofold commitment:

1. To magnify Jesus Christ (Philippians 1:20-22).
2. The good of others (Philippians 1:24-26).

To magnify Christ and bring good to others is another way of understanding what it means to love the Lord and to love others.

DAY TWENTY-SIX

Scripture Reading: John 14:6

Why did God not provide many ways of salvation? Is that really the right question to ask? The better question is, "Why did God provide any way of salvation at all?" After all, we are sinners that have fallen short of God's glory and incurred His displeasure. However, in the kindness of God He has provided His Son to be the Savior of all who believe in Him. It was all of grace that God chose to make a way for sinful man to be reconciled to Himself.

It is essential to understand that there is only one way, one path, one road that leads to God. Such thinking flies in the face of common opinion. It is widely believed that all religions offer various pathways that lead to God.

There is some truth to that. What I mean is that all people will stand before God. Some will stand before Him condemned. Others will stand before Him having come through faith in Christ.

When someone intimates that all roads lead to God, they are thinking that at the end of life everyone ends up in the same good and comforting place.

The Bible says that Jesus is the one and only way to God. You cannot get to God by being good enough, religious enough or avoiding sin enough. Salvation is not about your goodness. If you are to be saved then you must go through Jesus Christ. The fact that God has provided His Son as the way of salvation is the ultimate reason for giving thanks.

Historical Glimpse

The first National Thanksgiving Proclamation was given by the Continental Congress on November 1st, 1777.

This proclamation spoke of the duty of all men to:

1. Adore the God of providence.
2. Acknowledge with gratitude their obligation to Him for benefits received.
3. Ask Him for all blessings that they need.

The proclamation called upon the people to pray *God would shine upon us in the prosecution of a just and necessary war...to prosper the means used for the support of our troops and to crown our army with most signal success.*

The proclamation continued with a call to repentance and prayer that it may please God through the merits of Jesus Christ mercifully to forgive them.

The date for the National Thanksgiving was to be December 18th.

It is striking to note that the Continental Congress was very specific as to the God to whom they were praying and the way to God through Jesus Christ. This proclamation contained no minimalist and generalized statements about God. It was concise, clear and perhaps was used by God to bring conviction to the people.

One place to read this proclamation is:
http://www.pilgrimhall.org/GivingThanks3c.htm

Theological Thought

When giving thanks to God, it is essential to draw attention to the character of God as described in the Bible. Many people profess a faith in God but speak of God primarily in generic terms. We can only approach God through the merits of Jesus Christ. Jesus is the only way to the Father (John 14:6). We must be specific as we lead our children in the worship of God and as we witness to our neighbors. There are not many pathways to God. There is only one and that path is paved by the merits of Jesus Christ.

If salvation is only through Jesus then it is essential that we know who Jesus is. The Bible gives us that answer.

When you witness to someone about Christ make sure that your testimony is saturated with Scripture. It is important to take the time to explain who Jesus is, what He has done and how to be reconciled with Him.

Focus on the work of Christ and give thanks!

DAY TWENTY-SEVEN

Scripture Reading: Ephesians 5:20

*Over the next several days the "Historical Glimpse" contains excerpts from several Presidential Thanksgiving Proclamations. The source that I used was www.pilgrimhall.org. However, the Proclamations can be found at a variety of places on the Internet.

Notice in the Scripture reading two very important words, "always" and "everything." Thanksgiving is not to be an occasional expression but is to be evident in the Christians heart "always." Thanksgiving is not simply reserved for times of great blessings but also in seasons of loss, grief and heartbreak.

Historical Glimpse

THANKSGIVING DAY 1789 BY THE PRESIDENT OF THE UNITED STATES OF AMERICA - A PROCLAMATION

Whereas it is the duty of all Nations to acknowledge the providence of almighty God, to obey his will, to be grateful for his benefits, and humbly to implore his protection and favor - and Whereas both Houses of Congress have by their joint Committee requested me "to recommend to the People of the United States a day of public thanksgiving and prayer to be observed by acknowledging with grateful hearts the many signal favors of Almighty God, especially by affording them an opportunity peaceably to establish a form of government for their safety and happiness." Now therefore I do recommend and assign Thursday the 26th day of November next to be devoted by the People of these States to the service of that great and glorious Being, who is the beneficent Author of all the good that was, that is, or that will be – That we may then all unite in rendering unto him our sincere and humble thanks – for his kind care and protection of the People of this country previous to their becoming a Nation – for the signal and manifold mercies, and the favorable interpositions of his providence, which we experienced in the course and conclusion of the late war –for the great degree of tranquility, union, and plenty, which we have since enjoyed – for the peaceable and rational manner in which we have been enabled to establish constitutions of government for our safety and happiness, and particularly the national One now lately instituted, for the civil and religious liberty with which we are blessed, and the means we have of acquiring and diffusing useful knowledge; and in general for all the great and various favors which he hath been pleased to confer upon us. And also that we may then unite in most humbly offering our prayers and supplications to the great Lord and Ruler of Nations and beseech him to pardon our national and other transgressions – to enable us all, whether in public or private stations, to perform our several and relative duties properly and punctually – to render our national government a blessing to all the People, by constantly being a government of wise, just, and constitutional laws, discreetly and faithfully executed and obeyed – to protect and guide all Sovereigns and Nations (especially such as have shewn kindness unto us) and to bless them with good government, peace, and concord – To promote the knowledge and practice of true religion and virtue, and the increase of science among them and Us – and generally to grant unto all mankind such a degree of temporal prosperity as he alone knows to be best. Given under my hand at the City of New York the third day of October in the year of our Lord 1789.

George Washington, President

It is interesting to note that though President Washington had many substantive things to say, his proclamation was not nearly as theologically specific as the one from the Continental Congress.

Theological Glimpse

Washington's proclamation contains both direct and indirect references to providence. The providence of God, as we have learned, is His superintendence over His creation including how He directs all things in accordance to His will. Washington notes the importance of seeking His "protection and favor" to have grateful hearts for His favor. He also deals with sin but not as specifically and directly as did the first proclamation by the Continental Congress.

Indeed let us give thanks to God and seek His favor. Let us cry out in repentance for our sins both individually and nationally, and let us pray that we will be faithful in all our duties.

Providence, prayer, thanksgiving, repentance and duty are some of the theological themes that are sounded in Washington's address.

DAY TWENTY-EIGHT

Scripture Reading: Psalm 116:17

Prayer and thanksgiving are connected in Scripture. In fact thanksgiving is an element of prayer. Some have found it helpful to use this acrostic as a teaching aid for prayer:

A: Adoration
C: Confession
*T: **Thanksgiving***
S. Supplication

Read Philippians 4:5 to see another passage where prayer and thanksgiving are listed together.

Historical Glimpse

Lincoln's proclamation of 1863 is probably the best-known Thanksgiving proclamation. The nation was at war—North against South. The scars of war were deep and wide. Lincoln's proclamation no doubt brought comfort to a suffering nation. It also was the first of what would become an annual tradition in our country. Every President after Lincoln would follow his example and issue a proclamation just prior to Thanksgiving.

The year that is drawing toward its close has been filled with the blessings of fruitful fields and healthful skies. To these bounties, which are so constantly enjoyed that we are prone to forget the source from which they come, others have been added which are of so extraordinary a nature that they cannot fail to penetrate and soften even the heart, which is habitually insensible to the ever-watchful providence of Almighty God. In the midst of a civil war of unequaled magnitude and severity, which has sometimes seemed to foreign states to invite and to provoke their aggression, peace has been preserved with all nations, order has been maintained, the laws have been respected and obeyed, and harmony has prevailed everywhere, except in the theater of military conflict, while that theater has been greatly contracted by the advancing armies and navies of the Union. Needful diversions of wealth and of strength from the fields of peaceful industry to the national defense have not arrested the plow, the shuttle, or the ship; the ax has enlarged the borders of our settlements, and the mines, as well of iron and coal as of the precious metals, have yielded even more abundantly than heretofore. Population has steadily increased notwithstanding the waste that has been made in the camp, the siege, and the battlefield, and the country, rejoicing in the consciousness of augmented strength and vigor, is permitted to expect continuance of years with large increase of freedom. No human counsel hath devised nor hath any mortal hand worked out these great things. They are the gracious gifts of the Most High God, who, while dealing with us in anger for our sins, hath nevertheless remembered mercy. It has seemed to me fit and proper that they should be solemnly, reverently, and gratefully acknowledged, as with one heart and one voice, by the whole American people. I do therefore invite my fellow-citizens in every part of the United States, and also those who are at sea and those who are sojourning in foreign lands, to set apart and observe the last Thursday of November next as a day of thanksgiving and praise to our beneficent Father who dwelleth in the heavens. And I recommend to them that while offering up the ascriptions justly due to Him for such singular deliverances and blessings they do also, with humble penitence for our national perverseness and disobedience, commend to His tender care all those who have become widows, orphans, mourners, or sufferers in the lamentable civil strife in which we are unavoidably engaged, and fervently implore the interposition of the Almighty hand to heal the wounds of the nation and to restore if, as soon as may be consistent with the divine purpose, to the full enjoyment of peace, harmony, tranquility, and union. In testimony whereof I have hereunto set my hand and caused the seal of the United States to be affixed. Done at the city of Washington, this 3d day of October A.D. 1863, and of the Independence of the United States the eighty-eighth.

President Abraham Lincoln 1863

Theological Thought

Nostalgia is a longing for things past and may carry with it a sense of hopelessness. The Bible challenges us to look back and remember the blessings of God. Such remembering is different from nostalgia in that it is designed to strengthen faith and build hope. How did God's people respond to His faithfulness in history? That is a great question to consider. Just as we draw confidence from what we know to be true about God, we also learn from both the positive and negative responses to God from His people. The Bible presents man as fallen and in need of His grace. Even the heroes of the Bible are presented in their sinfulness.

It is appropriate to look back and remember the blessings of God. To remember God is both a present responsibility and brings a future hope. As Lincoln said, "We are prone to forget the source from which they (our blessings) come."

"Praise God from Whom All Blessings Flow..." goes the famous doxology that is featured prominently in many Sunday worship services. Let us never forget to praise our great God who is the giver of every good gift.

God in His anger has nevertheless remembered mercy. Let us remember God in all of His attributes as we give Him thanks.

DAY TWENTY-NINE

Scripture Reading: Daniel 2:23

Daniel is remembered for his convictions about prayer. "To you O God of my fathers, I give thanks..." Daniel thanked God (the object of all true thanksgiving) for granting wisdom, might and answered prayer.

To the person who truly understands the gift and opportunities of prayer they cannot but help to give thanks unto the Lord.

Historical Glimpse

THANKSGIVING DAY - 1902 BY THE PRESIDENT OF THE UNITED STATES OF AMERICA - A PROCLAMATION

... Over a century and a quarter has passed since this country took its place among the nations of the earth, and during that time we have had, on the whole, more to be thankful for than has fallen to the lot of any other people. Generation after generation has grown to manhood and passed away. Each has had to bear its peculiar burdens, each to face its special crisis, and each has known cares of grim trial, when the country was menaced by malice domestic or foreign levy, when the hand of the

Lord was heavy upon it in drought or flood or pestilence, when in bodily distress and in anguish of soul it paid the penalty of folly and a forward heart. Nevertheless, decade-by-decade we have struggled onward and upward; we now abundantly enjoy material well being, and under the favor of the Most High we are striving earnestly to achieve moral and spiritual uplifting. The year that has just closed has been one of peace and of overflowing plenty. Rarely have any people enjoyed greater prosperity than we are now enjoying. For this we render heartfelt thanks to the giver of Good; and we will seek to praise Him, not by words only, but by deeds, by the way in which we do our duty to ourselves and to our fellow-men. Now, wherefore, I, Theodore Roosevelt, President of the United States, do hereby designate as a day of general thanksgiving, Thursday, the twenty-seventh of the coming November, and do recommend that throughout the land the people cease from their ordinary occupations, and in their several homes and places of worship render thanks unto Almighty God for the manifold blessings of the past year...

THEODORE ROOSEVELT

Theological Thought

What are the sorts of things that the Christian should pray for?

1. Wisdom (Daniel 2:23).
2. Protection from the wiles of the devil (Luke 22:31-32, 40).
3. For God's will (Luke 22:42).

Prayer is a God-provided means of drawing near to God. In prayer He allows us to approach Him through Jesus Christ and bring our cries, our hopes, dreams, requests, concerns and everything else. He is able to shoulder our burdens and care for our needs.

There are many challenges to prayer including the weakness of our bodies, the distractions of our minds and the ongoing battle that we face with sin. The Christian can grow apathetic and lose confidence in God. When the heart grows colder the Christian must gird himself up and seek God in prayer. Let him repent of his cold heart and ask God for a heart burning with God-honoring passion. The deeper we go in prayer the more we will desire the knowledge of God. The more we know God the greater our capacity to seek His will.

DAY THIRTY

Scripture Reading: I Corinthians 11:24

The Lord's Supper is a meal during which we remember the great work of Christ on behalf of His people. It is also an occasion for giving thanks to the Lord for His body and His blood that was given for His people. As Jesus transformed the Passover Meal to the Lord's Supper, He gave thanks. His example of thanksgiving is a reminder to us all to remember our Lord and to give Him thanks.

Historical Glimpse

THANKSGIVING DAY, 1981 Proclamation 4883. November 12, 1981 BY THE PRESIDENT OF THE UNITED STATES OF AMERICA, A PROCLAMATION

America has much for which to be thankful. The unequaled freedom enjoyed by our citizens has provided a harvest of plenty to this nation throughout its history. In keeping with America's heritage, one day each year is set aside for giving thanks to God for all of His blessings. On this day of thanksgiving, it is appropriate that we recall the first thanksgiving, celebrated in the autumn of 1621. After surviving a bitter winter, the Pilgrims planted and harvested a bountiful crop. After the harvest they gathered their families together and joined in celebration and prayer with the Native Americans who had taught them so much. Clearly our forefathers were thankful not only for the material well-being of their harvest but for this abundance of goodwill as well. In this spirit, Thanksgiving has become a day when Americans extend a helping hand to the less fortunate. Long before there was a government welfare program, this spirit of voluntary giving was ingrained in the American character. Americans have always understood that, truly, one must give in order to receive. This should be a day of giving as well as a day of thanks. As we celebrate Thanksgiving in 1981, we should reflect on the full meaning of this day as we enjoy the fellowship that is so much a part of the holiday festivities. Searching our hearts, we should ask what we could do as individuals to demonstrate our gratitude to God for all He has done. Such reflection can only add to the significance of this precious day of remembrance. Let us recommit ourselves to that devotion to God and family that has played such an important role in making this a great Nation, and which will be needed as a source of strength if we are to remain a great people...

RONALD REAGAN

Theological Thought

We have so much for which to be thankful. Many times the focus is on what we possess, where we live, and the freedoms that we enjoy. Indeed, we should be thankful to God for all of these things.

President Reagan pointed out that the Pilgrims were thankful "not only for the material well-being of their harvest but for this abundance of goodwill as well (referring to the good will expressed to them by their Indian friends).

President Reagan went on to remind Americans of their responsibility to give help to others as they give thanks to God.

He then challenges Americans to:
1. Search their hearts.
2. Ask what we can do to demonstrate our gratitude to God for all that He has done.
3. Recommit to devotion to God and family.

Would it not be wise to heed President Reagan's challenge? Examine your heart! Ask God what you can do to better show your thanksgiving. Recommit your life to the pursuit of God and call your family to do the same.

DAY THIRTY-ONE

Scripture Reading: 2 Corinthians 9:15

Paul speaks of giving thanks to God for "His indescribable gift." The gift he is referring to is salvation. Probably most of the people reading this book have been blessed with all that they need concerning food, clothes, shelter, and transportation. We often express our thanksgiving for these things. But how often do we reflect deeply and then give genuine thanks to God for the indescribable gift that He has given us in His Son Jesus.

Historical Sketch

Thanksgiving Day 2008 November 21, 2008 A Proclamation by the President of the United States of America

Thanksgiving is a time for families and friends to gather together and express gratitude for all that we have been given, the freedoms we enjoy, and the loved ones who enrich our lives. We recognize that all of these blessings, and life itself, come not from the hand of man but from Almighty God. Every Thanksgiving, we remember the story of the Pilgrims who came to America in search of religious freedom and a better life. Having arrived in the New World, these early settlers gave thanks to the *Author of Life for granting them safe passage to this abundant land and protecting them through a bitter winter. Our Nation's first President, George Washington, stated in the first Thanksgiving proclamation that "It is the duty of all nations to acknowledge the providence of Almighty God, to obey His will, to be grateful for His benefits, and humbly to implore His protection and favor." While in the midst of the Civil War, President Abraham Lincoln revived the tradition of proclaiming a day of thanksgiving, asking God to heal our wounds and restore our country. Today, as we look back on the beginnings of our democracy, Americans recall that we live in a land of many blessings where every person has the right to live, work, and worship in freedom. Our Nation is especially thankful for the brave men and women of our Armed Forces who protect these rights while setting aside their own comfort and safety. Their courage keeps us free, their sacrifice makes us grateful, and their character makes us proud. Especially during the holidays, our whole country keeps them and their families in our thoughts and prayers.*

Americans are also mindful of the need to share our gifts with others, and our Nation is moved to compassionate action. We pay tribute to all caring citizens who reach out a helping hand and serve a cause larger than themselves. On this day, let us all give thanks to God who blessed our Nation's first days and who blesses us today. May He continue to guide and watch over our families and our country always...

GEORGE W. BUSH

President Bush, in all of his Thanksgiving proclamations remembered the Pilgrims and their first Thanksgiving.

He remembered to thank God for those who serve in the Armed Forces. It was during the War Between the States that our first annual National Thanksgiving Proclamation was issued by President Lincoln. There was no way that either the Confederate or Federal governments could provide an official Thanksgiving celebration for their troops. However, some troops in different areas did band together to give thanks to God.

"Thanksgiving 1864 did not go similarly unrecognized. The Union League Club of New York City launched a public campaign to provide Thanksgiving dinner for Union soldiers and sailors:

We desire that on the twenty-fourth day of November there shall be no soldier in the Army of the Potomac, the James, the Shenandoah, and no sailor in the North Atlantic Squadron who does not receive tangible evidence that those for whom he is periling his life, remember him...

We ask primarily for donations of cooked poultry and other proper meats, as well as for mince pies, sausages and fruits... To those who are unable to send donations in kind, we appeal for generous contributions in money.

The response was overwhelming. In 3 weeks, the Club collected over $57,000 towards the purchase of 146,586 pounds of poultry. Donations of an additional 225,000 pounds of poultry were received, along with an enormous quantity of other meat, cakes, gingerbread, pickles, apples, vegetables, cheese, and mince pies."

Captain George F. Noyes reported from General Phil Sheridan's Army of the Shenandoah:

The want of proper appliances compelled most of the men to broil or stew their turkeys, but everyone seemed fully satisfied, and appreciated the significance of this sympathetic thank-offering from the loyal North. One

*soldier said to me, "It isn't the turkey, but the **idea** that we care for,"
and he thus struck the key-note of the whole festival.*[50]

Theological Thought

The Bible teaches concerning governmental authority:
*For he is God's servant for your good. But if you do wrong, be
afraid, for he does not bear the sword in vain. For he is the servant
of God, an avenger who carries out God's wrath on the wrong-
doer" (Romans 13:4).*

It is the responsibility of those with governmental
authority to defend, protect and to punish evildoers. The
book of Romans was written during a time when Rome
was ruling the world and in no sense could Rome be
referred to as a "Christian nation." However, Christians
were to be submissive and to recognize the authority of
the government to "bear the sword."

Godly Christians have debated the question of war
throughout history. The weight of the biblical evidence
seems to be that though war is always a result of sin, that
war is one way in which wickedness is restrained, people
are protected, and order is preserved. It is not prudent
that a nation should beat the drums of war and rush to
the battlefield. However, when necessary a nation
should be willing to go to war. Throughout history war
has been discussed in terms of a just or unjust war. A
just war is a war that is deemed to be justifiable along
biblical principles.

During times of war Christians should be thankful for
those willing to make the ultimate sacrifice for the well-

being of their fellow citizens. The holiday seasons are especially good times to pray for fellow church members and friends that are far from home in their service to God via their service to their nation.

Sarah Josepha Hale wrote:

Are not the sounds of war borne on the breezes of those festivals (Washington's Birthday and the Fourth of July)? One comes in the cold of winter; the other in the heat of summer; while the glorious autumn of the year, when blessings are gathered in, has no day of remembrance for her gifts of peace. Should not the women of America have one festival in whose rejoicings they can fully participate?[51]

Sarah Hale believed that a national Thanksgiving Day could help to unify the nation that, just prior to 1861, was on the brink of war. She saw Thanksgiving as an opportunity to bring peace in the midst of anger and she believed that Thanksgiving would remember the "gifts of peace" of autumn.

In times of war let us give thanks to God for His protection through those that risk their lives and suffer great hardship. Let us also give Him thanks that even in the midst of war that through Jesus Christ we have peace. Let us also take the opportunity to use Thanksgiving Day as a day to promote peace and goodwill.

More Thoughts on Thanksgiving

Lydia Maria Child started the first children's magazine in America. She is well known for her poem: *Over the river and through the wood...* This was her Thanksgiving song. It was originally titled *The New England Boy's Song: About Thanksgiving Day.* She wrote twelve verses to this song, most of which are not sung today. The song was published in 1845 in her book, *Flowers for Children.*

The song is reflective of the spirit of Child and of Sarah Hale. Thanksgiving was about giving thanks to God and about unity. Both Hale and Child desired a unity of family and nation. Both nation and family were rapidly changing in the mid 1800's.

With increased ability to travel many people were leaving the place of their birth. It was increasingly difficult to make a living on the family farm, and with the growth of business and industry, many in the younger generation found employment away from home.

The nation itself was divided. There had always been the debates over the role of the central government verses the rights of the individual states. With the western expansion of the country, those debates intensified and increasingly focused on the issue of slavery. Slavery had never been simply a Southern problem. It was a national problem. Slavery was not the sole reason for national unrest. The nation was expanding, and technology was advancing. The strong Christian foundation held by many of the early settlers of the country increasingly was challenged by deism, Unitarianism and civil religion.

The national unrest had political, social and even religious facets. The nation was facing growing pains and seeking to discover what kind of nation she would be.

Sarah Hale believed that a national Thanksgiving Day proclaimed by the president and adopted by all of the States could be a help to bringing the nation and individual families together.

Penny Colman writes, *Why was Sarah Josepha Hale so passionate about Thanksgiving? Undoubtedly growing up in New England where an annual autumn Thanksgiving Day was already well established influenced her. For her, it was a special time for families to attend church together and share a feast. She was also responding to the dramatic transformation of the United States. In such tumultuous times, Hale believed that a national Thanksgiving Day had much to offer America. Her vision was of all Americans 'uniting as one Great Family Republic.' She believed that celebrating a national Thanksgiving Day would 'awaken in American hearts, the love of home and country, of thankfulness to God, and peace between brethren.*[52]

Next time you sing, "Over the river..." you will know the sentiment that both Lydia Maria Child and Sarah

Josepha Hale felt about the need for togetherness. Thanksgiving Day was one way such family and national unity could be promoted.

> *Over the river, and through the wood,*
> *To grandfather's house we go;*
> *The horse knows the way,*
> *To carry the sleigh,*
> *Through the white and drifted snow.*
>
> *Over the river, and through the wood,*
> *To grandfather's house away!*
> *We would not stop*
> *For doll or top,*
> *For 'tis Thanksgiving Day...*

Colman writes, *With families scattered, many people must have felt a longing for one another, a longing that undoubtedly prompted them to embrace the idea of a holiday that brought everyone home.*[53]

In November of 1856 a poem was published in *The Youth's Companion* that also reflects the desire for family unity.

> *Come, uncles and cousins; come, nieces and aunts;*
> *Come, nephews and brothers,—no wonts and no cants;*
> *Put business, and shopping, and school-books away;*
> *The year has rolled around;—it is Thanksgiving-day.*
>
> *Come home from the college, ye ringlet-haired youth,*
> *Come home from your factories, Ann, Kate, and Ruth;*
> *From the anvil, the counter, the farm come away;*
> *Home, home with you, home;—it is Thanksgiving-Day*[54]

Gospel Thoughts

True unity is only possible through Christ. As a Christian, Sarah Hale no doubt recognized that indisputable fact. External unity and a patriotic brotherhood, even when they are best promoted and realized, cannot long last because without Christ they have no foundation, no fuel to empower and no ultimate purpose towards which to aim. It is foolish to hope that we might all just get along, join hands and celebrate Thanksgiving Day unless we are Christ focused and gospel driven. That being said Christians believe in "common grace." God brings rain and sunshine on Christians and non-Christians alike. As Christians we are to spread kindness as we go through life. In that sense, the promotion of a national celebration that reminds all of their duty to give thanks to God is appropriate. It is this thinking that has driven Christians to promote the work of hospitals, schools, orphanages and even national celebrations. I think this is the spirit in which Christians should view such a day as Thanksgiving. The togetherness of friends, family and others is another way of spreading God's common grace on all people.

The great sin of fallen man is a failure to worship God. This sin involves suppressing the truth and not honoring nor giving thanks to God (Romans 1:18-32). On the one hand, Thanksgiving Day provides an opportunity to remind all people of their duty to give thanks to God. It is also an opportunity to be reminded of the fact that in the midst of great blessing, we have often failed individually and as a nation to give God that which He so deserves—thanksgiving. There is, then, a great gospel opportunity on Thanksgiving Day. As we declare the duty of all to give thanks we also reject the sin of not giving thanks. We then should declare the gospel. Through Jesus Christ the demands that God requires are met by His righteous life, substitutionary death and bodily resurrection.

Our Duty: Give thanks.
Our Sin: We have not acknowledged, loved and given thanks to God.
Our Need: Christ as the One who has fulfilled the demands of God's law through His righteous life, atoning death and resurrection.
Our Response: Repent and believe the gospel. Faith in Christ is by grace. Once a person turns from sin (repentance) and turns to God (faith in Christ) the Holy Spirit comes to live in their heart enabling them to live for Christ. The Christian then spends the rest of his life pursuing obedience while trusting in Christ and being empowered by the Spirit. Once a person is saved by grace his eyes are opened to see the goodness of God then to give thanks.

If you have never been delivered from your sins and reconciled to God, then let me encourage you right now to seek God in prayer, repent of your sins, ask God for the faith to trust in His Son for salvation, believe on the Lord Jesus Christ and give God thanks. It is also vitally important that you find a church where the Bible is proclaimed and participate with fellow Christians in the worship of God.

Thanksgiving Day is a wonderful celebration that, at least for a time, promotes national and family unity. However, do not put too much hope in such a day or effort. The great need of our nation is not more holidays; the great need of our nation is a spiritual awakening to the greatness of God and a corresponding humility, repentance, faith and life of thanksgiving.

As Christians we might promote and celebrate the day as Sarah Hale did. But like her we must also look to the greater needs of the nation and her families by proclaiming the gospel of our Lord.

Thanksgiving Musings

As our nation developed and prospered, some of the original focus of earlier Thanksgiving Days began to diminish. The earlier emphasis on God and His providence was redirected to a variety of social activities and games. Those things (socializing, games etc.) are not bad things, but over time they began to crowd out the central tenet of Thanksgiving—to give thanks to God.

Though America has always had deep and theologically strong Christian roots, she has been a mixed nation. Even on the *Mayflower* there were those not associated with the Pilgrims from a religious perspective who came to America for reasons other than worship. As the nation developed, expanded and prospered there came, in some cases, a religion more civic than specifically theological.

Increasingly, even family togetherness was threatened as special events outside of the home were promoted on Thanksgiving Day. In the 20th century the day more and more became associated with shopping and the beginning of Christmas. Though the day itself has avoided some of the commercialization of other holidays, it has become the diving board from which shoppers jump into the pool of Christmas.

Perhaps the focus of earlier Thanksgiving Days can be recovered. Years of Thanksgiving memories are etched in my mind. My wife, Lori and I have sought to instill within our children the value of traditions. We see Thanksgiving and Christmas as opportunities for our children to be reminded of the historical context of our family. We are not isolated individuals at the center of the universe. We are members of a family and stand upon the shoulders of others. Several generations gather on Thanksgiving Day. The old and the young come together for a meal, laughs and to be reminded again of the ties that bind.

The children will remember when grandparents clasped their little hands. They will remember running across the yard laughing and playing. They will also remember the times of grief when loved ones have been sick or have died or when there is a missing family member that could not make it to the annual celebration. They will remember. They will stand on their memories and build their own traditions as they marry and have children of their own.

Family traditions, marked by gatherings, are treasured. However, what we most want our children to know and remember is that the family we have, the life we live, the blessings we enjoy are gifts from our benevolent God. It is our prayer that such reminders of His goodness will lead them to repentance and faith in Christ as they learn God's Word.

I am writing this series of family worship books because by God's sweet grace I am blessed with a family. We are fallen, broken and in constant need of repair. However, God is our God and we want to better worship Him. His Word teaches us to value the lessons of history. There are lessons that my children need—that I need. After all this is our Father's world. Standing upon the inerrant foundation of His Word we can then interpret and learn the lessons from all of history.

Soon it will be time for the turkey and dressing. Sweet and Irish potatoes will be prepared. The pies will be placed in the oven and one by one the families will arrive. At the end of the day—just prior to going to bed—take your copy of the Bible and read. It is always right to give thanks to the Lord. It is not only right; it is His will. Let this Thanksgiving season remind you to give thanks in all things—always!

Sarah Hale On Thanksgiving

"The moral effect of this simple festival is essentially good. It is a season of grateful joy in view of the rich blessings of Providence, which has thus crowned the year with its goodness. It is a part of the noble patrimony of our Puritan Fathers. Blessed be their memories! May their stern, uncompromising integrity—their deep piety which pervaded all their thoughts, feelings and actions, running through all their institutions—their simplicity of character—their devoted love of country—their fearless support of religious liberty—may these virtues ever be the inheritance, the guard, the guide, and guerdon of their descendants. The Puritans stamped themselves for good upon the institutions which they established, and the habits and customs, which they formed and transmitted, to their descendants. And this spirit has gone out over our whole country, more or less, and has fashioned and modified the American character. "

http://www.pilgrimhall.org/ThanksSarahJosepha7.htm

Family Activities

A "Thankful" Book

During the Thanksgiving season, while gathering with your family, take the time to chronicle what is happening. Use a blank book and write down family expressions of thanksgiving. Make it a personal "Thankful" book and let everyone write or draw and include what they like. Be sure to include Scripture verses or hymns that have been an encouragement to your family. Get a good quality book with sufficient pages to add your memories to each year. Share your book with friends and extended family at your Thanksgiving gathering. Your "Thankful" book will likely become an instant classic.

Other activities that could be incorporated in your family worship could include:

Sing Hymns – We sing a hymn every morning during our devotions before school and read about the hymn or its author. What a joy it is during church for one of the little ones to look up and smile realizing that they know the hymn and something about it. Some of our favorite Thanksgiving hymns are *Great is Thy Faithfulness, It Is Well, Come Ye Thankful People, For the Beauty of the Earth* and *We Gather Together.*

Write out Scripture Verses – We have a folder full of verses the girls wrote out and decorated one year. Give your children blank paper and colored pencils and they will create a masterpiece worthy to be sent to grandparents, nursing homes and anyone who needs encouragement.

Make placards – You can begin ahead of time and make place cards that will be placed at every person's seat. Be creative, write Scripture on each card to be read aloud at your meals, make them in fun shapes like turkeys. This is directly related to Thanksgiving and you can go online and look for patterns to make. One year we made tiny turkeys out of clay pots with two different church groups and our extended family. We wrote everyone's names on them and had really fun gifts to give as they left.

Pray – This goes without saying. Ask for prayer requests, and then pray! Be specific and remember that no request is too small or too great for our God who reigns. We can help those in need by praying for them (read 2 Corinthians 1:11).

Afterword: Lori Rhodes

Our traditions of Thanksgiving bring sweet memories--lunch with Ray's family, group pictures, football in the front yard, Nana's turkey and dressing, a meal with my family sometime over the holiday weekend and numerous other blessings. It is rare that we see loved ones all together in the same place at the same time, except during one of the major holidays. Therefore we use this opportunity to share our faith with family. As we gather together we look for opportunities to read Scripture aloud and give a gospel witness. There is also the time of prayer that precedes the Thanksgiving meal. We lead our children to think about the greatness of God and all He has done for us. Going beyond "God is great, God is good, let us thank Him for our food," this is the time to count our blessings.

The Thanksgiving season is a time in which my senses come alive. Each holiday has it's own sights, sounds and smells. Thanksgiving is no different. The aroma of this holiday has developed over the years, beginning in early fall with apples cooking and a trip to the pumpkin farm. Well before the "big" day, pies start filling up the freezer − chocolate, pumpkin and pecan. And what can beat the smells of the turkey cooking all night and waking to fresh biscuits and cornbread that are used to make the dressing? Those are smells that celebrate God's bounty.

The sounds of Thanksgiving are like music to my ears-laughing children, clinking dishes, football on the television, pots banging and balls bouncing. Even the sound of Ray saying, "Ya'll leave those dishes, I'll get them later." Everyone knows by much experience that Ray's comments about the dishes are not to be taken seriously. There are so many conversations going at the same time there is no way to follow any of them coherently.

My tastes of Thanksgiving have evolved over the years also. When I was a teenager I don't remember trying pumpkin. Now it is one of my favorites in pie, muffins, and rolls. I always enjoyed the turkey and dressing, but now I appreciate it so much more. Early in my marriage I received a chocolate pie recipe from a dear friend of our family, Mr. Bill, and it has become a staple for the holidays. We always make an extra one of those and hide it for Ray's brother Andrew to take home.

The feelings of love and family that flow at Thanksgiving are part of who we are. We love on each other, share in preparations and clean up together. We cry together and tell each other secrets. How fun it is to be squeezed into those family pictures that represent so much more than how tall the children have gotten. They tell the story of God's faithfulness in family love, blessings and even grief over loss. The photographs represent one more year with those we love and another opportunity to praise God for His bountiful blessings.

As your family gathers to celebrate Thanksgiving Day, don't forget to remember God. Laying the foundation of thankfulness to God is the most important tradition to develop during this season.

Part of sharing holidays and special occasions is gathering recipes. Here are a few of our favorites.

Nana's Ohhh So Good Dressing

Mix together lots of fresh cornbread and biscuits (with buttermilk) that have been crumbled really fine with the juice from a giant turkey that cooked all night. Add in some chopped onions, a couple of eggs, some butter, salt and pepper until it all looks about right. Then cook it until it looks done. Yes, that's the recipe! No measuring cup needed.

Mr. Bill's Chocolate Pie

Melt together over medium heat 1 and ½ sticks of butter or margarine and 12 ounces of semisweet chocolate chips. In a separate bowl mix together 1 and ½ cups of sugar, 4 eggs beaten, ½ cup of chopped pecans. Then pour chocolate mixture into this and mix well. Pour everything into 2 pie shells, slightly cooked. Top with more pecans if desired and bake at 300 degrees for about 45 minutes. Pies are done when they are no longer jiggly in the center.

Laurie Sealock's Streusel Topped Pumpkin Muffins

1/4 cup softened butter   1/2 cup sugar   1/4 cup brown sugar   2/3 cup pumpkin   1/2 cup buttermilk   2 eggs   2 tbsp molasses   1 tsp grated orange peel   2 cup flour   2 tsp baking powder   1 tsp baking soda   1 tsp pumpkin pie spice   1/4 tsp salt (Streusel Topping   1/3 cup flour   3 tbsp brown sugar   2 tbsp cold butter)   Cream butter and sugars. Add pumpkin, buttermilk, eggs, molasses, orange peel. Mix well. Combine dry ingredients then gradually add to pumpkin mixture just until blended. Fill muffin cups 2/3 full. Mix ingredients for streusel topping until crumbly and sprinkle on top of muffins. Bake 20-25 minutes at 375 degrees. Cool in pan 5 minutes before removing.

End Notes

[1] Ruth E. Finley, *The Lady of Godey's: Sarah Josepha Hale* (Philadelphia and London: J.B. Lippincott Company, 1931, Sixth Printing), pp. 35-36

[2] Finley, p. 36

[3] Finley, p. 198

[4] Finley, pp. 198-199

[5] Finley, pp. 17-18

[6] www.pilgrimhall.org

[7] Sarah Josepha Hale, *Woman's Record: Sketches of all Distinguished Women* (New York: Harper and Brothers, 1853), pp. xlvi-xlvii

[8] William Bradford, *Of Plymouth Plantation* (San Antonio: The Vision Forum, Inc, 1998-2005), p. 48

[9] Paul Jehle, *Plymouth in The Words of Her Founders* (San Antonio: The Vision Forum, Inc, 2002), p. 10

[10] Jehle, p. 11

[11] William J. Bennett, *Our Sacred Honor* (New York: Simon and Schuster, 1997), p. 386

[12] Keith and Kristyn Getty, *Beneath the Cross of Jesus* (Thank You Music, 2005), www.gettymusic.com

[13] John MacArthur, *The MacArthur New Testament Commentary: Acts 1-12* (Chicago: Moody Press, 1994), pp.90-91

[14] Horton Davies, *The Worship of the American Puritans* (Morgan, PA: Soli Deo Gloria, 1999.), pp. 68-69

[15] Jeremiah Burroughs, *The Rare Jewel of Christian Contentment* (Edinburgh: The Banner of Truth Trust, 2005), pp. 170-175

[16] Charles H. Spurgeon, *The Treasury of David, Vol.II* (McLean, Virginia: Macdonald Publishing Company), p. 233

[17] Spurgeon, p. 234

[18] Penny Colman, *Thanksgiving: The True Story* (New York: Henry Holt and Company, 2008), pp. 57-58

[19] Bradford, p.1

20 Bradford, p.8
21 Bradford, p.8
22 Bradford, p.23
23 Deborah Howard, *Where is God in All of This* (Phillipsburg, New Jersey: Presbyterian and Reformed Publishers, 2009), p. 152
24 Howard, p. 152
25 Bradford, p.17
26 Bradford, p.20
27 Bradford, p.21
28 Bradford, pp. 24-26
29 Bradford, p.48
30 E. Brooks Smith and Robert Meredith, *Pilgrim Courage* (Boston: Little, Brown and Company, 1962), pp. 19-20
31 Bradford, p.31
32 Bradford, p.55-56
33 Bradford, p.56
34 Bradford, p.63
35 Bradford, p.64
36 Bradford, p.65
37 Smith and Meredith, p.27
38 Smith and Meredith, p. 27
39 Bradford, pp. 72-74
40 Smith and Meredith, p. 59
41 James Janeway and Cotton Mather, *A Token For Children* (Morgan, PA: Soli Deo Gloria Publications, 1995), p. x
42 Smith and Meredith, p. 71
43 Bradford, pp. 82-83
44 Bradford, p.89
45 Smith and Meredith, pp. 95-96
46 Bradford, p.96
47 Jehle, pp. 53-54
48 Jehle, p. 60
49 Jehle, p. 61
50 From the Web-Site www.pilgrimhall.org
51 Coleman, p.49
52 Coleman, p.49
53 Coleman, p.49
54 Coleman, p.84

The Thanksgiving Proclamations used in this book came from www.pilgrimhall.org There you will find all of the Proclamations in full as well as an outstanding summary of Thanksgiving, Sarah Josepha Hale, The Pilgrims and much more from early American history.

**Information about the Pilgrims, Thanksgiving and other historical material not foot noted is considered common knowledge and is found in numerous sources. I chose to footnote information directly received from a source. Sources used do not necessarily constitute an endorsement. Any failures to properly document are the fault of the author and are unintended*

***All Biblical quotes are from the English Standard Version.*

Bibliography

Bennett, William. *Our Sacred Honor.* New York: Simon and Schuster, 1997. 430p.

Bradford, William. *Of Plymouth Plantation: Bradford's History of Plymouth Settlement 1608-1650.* San Antonio: The Vision Forum, 1998. 353p.

Burroughs, Jeremiah. *The Rare Jewel of Christian Contentment.* Carlisle, PA: Soli Deo Gloria, 2005. 228p.

Colman, Penny. *Thanksgiving: The True Story.* New York: Henry Holt and Company, 2008. 149p.

Davis, Horton. *The Worship of the American Puritans.* Morgan PA: Soli Deo Gloria, 1999. 338p.

Finley, Ruth. *The Lady of Godey's: Sarah Josepha Hale.* Philadelphia: J.B. Lippincott Company. 318p.

Howard, Deborah. *Where is God in All of This: Finding God's Purpose in Our Suffering.* Phillipsburg, NJ: Presbyterian and Reformed, 2009. 158p.

Jameway, James and Mather, Cotton. *A Token For Children.* Morgan, PA: Soli Deo Gloria, 1995. 146p.

Jehle, Paul. *Plymouth in the Words of Her Founders: A Visitor's Guide to America's Hometown.* San Antonio: The Vision Forum, 2002. 148p.

MacArthur, John. *The MacArthur New Testament Commentary: Acts 1-12.* Chicago: Moody, 1994. 341p.

Payne, Elizabeth. *Meet The Pilgrim Fathers.* New York: Random House, 1966. 86p.

Smith, Brooks, E. and Meredith, Robert. *Pilgrim Courage.* Boston: Little, Brown and Company, 1962. 108p.

Spurgeon, Charles. *The Treasury of David, Vol. II: Psalms 58-110.* McLean, Virginia: Macdonald Publishing Company, 479p.

www.pilgrimhall.org

COMMENDATIONS

"What a complete joy it is to offer my blessing and recommendation of Ray Rhodes', newest book, Family Worship for the Thanksgiving Season. Ray has given us a doxological feast of 31 creative lessons which offer the fruit of both an informed mind and enflamed heart. The beauty of Ray's writing may only be surpassed by the beauty of his family--the precious community in which our brother has invested so much of his heart and cultivated his tremendous love for the gospel and God's people. Not only your Thanksgiving season, but your entire year will be enriched by highly accessible and Biblically faithful reflections." Scotty Smith, Pastor for Preaching, Teaching and Worship Christ Community Church, Franklin TN, Author of Unveiled Hope, with Michael Card; Speechless, with Steven Curtis Chapman; Objects of His Affection; The Reign of Grace; and Restoring Broken Things, with Steven Curtis Chapman

"Ray Rhodes has provided another devotional gem that families who want to worship God in their homes will find useful. Though Thanksgiving tends to be more about travel, sporting events and food than about genuine gratitude to our Creator, the very name of the holiday provides an opportunity to stop and reflect on God's goodness. This book is an excellent guide in remembering God's mercies that are provided in the gospel while taking note of His kind providence in the history of America. Use it to stir up thanksgiving in your home as Thanksgiving approaches on your calendar."
- Dr. Tom Ascol, Executive Director Founders Ministries

"After reading this latest work by Ray Rhodes, I have never been more convinced that God has uniquely called him to write on Family Worship for our generation. His genuine burden is contagious and is being embraced by many at this needy hour. Could there be a better time in our nation's history for a Christian and his family to learn afresh or revisit the early moments of our nation's founding? Enter into the world of Pilgrim America. Relive that first Thanksgiving season. Follow our forefathers from Holland to Cape Cod. Then, emulate their faith. Pass it on to your children. And pray for God's mercy upon the USA." - Pastor Jerry Marcellino, Audubon Drive Bible Church, Laurel, Mississippi.

"In Family Worship for the Thanksgiving Season Ray Rhodes has provided families with a roadmap to thankfulness that includes some unique treasures not found in similar works. The combination of historic treasures that any Father or Mother can share with their children, in addition to theological pillars of our historic, Christian faith, each day is highlighted with a pertinent Scripture verse that ties it all together. This combination of Scripture, theology and history is rooted in our American tradition and heritage. Some works on the family tend to idolize the institution, thus making family the center of everything. Not so with Ray, for the family is set in its proper context of providing the foundation for character and devotion destined to bless both church and community through serving others and not indulging in self-gratification. This book will add another dimension to a family's knowledge and appreciation of our Thanksgiving tradition from the Pilgrims to the present day proclamations of Presidents who honored our forefathers. I highly recommend Family Worship!"- Dr. Paul Jehle, Senior Pastor, The New Testament Church, Plymouth, MA

About the Author

Ray Rhodes, Jr. is President of Nourished in the Word Ministries. Nourished in the Word is a teaching, writing, consulting and book ministry. Ray and Lori are blessed with five daughters: Rachel, Hannah, Sarah, Mary and Lydia. To schedule Ray to speak for your next event, please contact him at ray@nourishedintheword.org. Visit Lori Rhodes online at www.nitw4ladies.blogspot.com

Ray is the author of Family Worship for the Christmas Season, Family Worship for the Reformation Season, The Visionary Marriage and the soon to be released Family Worship for the Easter Season.

Ray and his family live in North Georgia.

CPSIA information can be obtained at www.ICGtesting.com
Printed in the USA
BVOW05s0827170414

350873BV00001B/29/P